1987

For Sally (& Mark) —
may these challenging
vignettes of our Lord
bring wisdom & comfort,
growth & assurance
as you walk in faith.

much love,
Karen & Don

THE OTHER
JESUS

THE OTHER JESUS

BY

LLOYD J. OGILVIE

WORD BOOKS
PUBLISHER
WACO, TEXAS

A DIVISION OF
WORD, INCORPORATED

All Scripture quotations, unless otherwise noted, are from The
Holy Bible, New King James Version, copyright © 1979,
1980, 1982 by Thomas Nelson, Inc. Used by permission. Scrip-
ture quotations marked RSV are from the Revised Standard
Version of the Bible, copyright © 1946, 1952, © 1971 and
1973 by the Division of Christian Education of the National
Council of the Churches of Christ in the U.S.A., and used
by permission. Scripture quotations marked NEB are from *The
New English Bible*, © 1961, 1970 by The Delegates of the Oxford
University Press and The Syndics of the Cambridge University
Press, and used by permission.

Library of Congress Cataloging in Publication Data

Ogilvie, Lloyd John.
  The Other Jesus:

  1. Jesus Christ—Person and offices.   2. Jesus
Christ—Words.   I. Title.
BT202.0325   1986   232   86–18996
ISBN 0–8499–0601–6

Printed in the United States of America

67898   FG   987654321

To
The Board of Directors of the
Let God Love You Television and Radio Ministry

for their commitment to communicate the other Jesus
for the deepest needs and most urgent questions
of the American people

ACKNOWLEDGMENTS

Deep appreciation is expressed to those who have made this book possible.

I am thankful that Floyd Thatcher, close friend and Editor-in-Chief at Word Books, edited the manuscript and helped me express more clearly what I have tried to communicate in this book. It's both a comfort and challenge to have a writer and thinker of Floyd's stature looking over my shoulder. He has been a mentor and fellow adventurer in the quest for excellence in communication.

Through the years, Pat Wienandt, Senior Academic Editor at Word, has been of immeasurable help in sharing the vision and purpose of many of my books. This has been especially true for this project. I have appreciated her enthusiasm for this book from the very beginning, all of her help along the way and her careful editing and preparation of the final manuscript for publication.

Nancy Moyer, my Executive Assistant, was responsible for overseeing the total project and guiding it to completion.

Lynne Beebe faithfully typed the manuscript through several revisions. The book would not have been completed on schedule without her tireless efforts at the word processor.

And special gratitude goes to George Bayz, friend and deacon in my church, who gives so much of this time and expertise to make the technology of computer science work to maximize all phases of my writing, church, and media ministries.

To all of these cherished friends, I express my appreciation and love.

LLOYD OGILVIE

CONTENTS

CHAPTER ONE

And they were astonished at His teaching, for He taught them
as one having authority, and not as the scribes.
(Mark 1:22)

THE OTHER JESUS

Who is this other Jesus? He is not a different Jesus. Rather, He is the forgotten, neglected, overlooked Jesus.

This other Jesus is often a stranger to our self-concerned, narcissistic, "me" generation. He's not the Jesus we've created of our own making and faking—an easy-going, good-natured Jesus who's on call when we want Him to help us deal with our personal agenda. Having only this culturalized, benevolent, but somewhat weak "errand-boy" Jesus stunts our spiritual growth. "It's a snivelling modern invention," says Shaw, "for which there is no warrant in the Gospels."

The other Jesus is the biblical Jesus—the robust, challenging Jesus, who is more than just a comforter. He also confronts us, and He will not accept second place in our lives. He calls us to the exhilarating adventure of dynamic discipleship.

Though He meets us as we are, He loves us too much to leave us as we've been.

The authentic Jesus tenderly cares for us when we hurt, but He tenaciously exposes anything that keeps us from being His faithful servants. His love and forgiveness are unqualified, but His demands are unequivocal. He is the Master who holds the mandate of the kingdom and the Lord of all life who calls us to commit all we have and are to Him.

The title of this chapter, "The Other Jesus," is not meant to be a clever attention-arrester. And it isn't meant to suggest an exposé about a recently discovered Jesus in some newly found scrolls or manuscripts. Instead, it is an honest recognition that contemporary Christianity, in its efforts to reach people where they hurt, has focused almost exclusively on a Jesus who is always available to solve our problems. That's fine for openers, but if that's all we know of Him, it can deny us of the greatness He desires for us.

Our needs do bring us to Jesus. It's wonderful to know Him as a Friend who will never leave or forsake us. He does sustain us when we are lonely, guide us when we are confused, and uplift us when we are discouraged. We do need Him when we fail, cry out for forgiveness, and long for reassurance. Yet we run the danger of limiting Jesus to being only our "problem-solver."

We can become like a friend of mine who relates to people on the basis of the most recent crisis of his life. The only time he calls or writes me is when he's facing a tough problem. When I see a note from him in my mail, sometimes I groan inside and wonder, "What does Sam want this time?"

Finally one day I asked Sam why he contacted me only when he was in trouble. He was perplexed and surprised by my question. But as we talked, he realized that all through his life he had felt that in order to get people's attention he had to have some kind of special need or crisis. The reason for his reaction soon became apparent. In thinking back to his boyhood, he remembered that the only time his parents seemed to pay attention to him was when he was in trouble. Through the years he projected that identical image onto his friends.

Then as we continued our conversation, Sam also came to see that he treated the Lord in the same way. His relationship to Him was pretty much limited to his problem times. Sam concentrated so much on his own agenda and needs that he never got to know or enjoy Jesus. And what's worse, Sam was so intent on getting Him to do what he wanted that he had missed the Lord's agenda for him.

Like Sam, we can become so preoccupied with getting Jesus to help us with our plans that we cannot hear the exciting plans He has for us. He calls us to attempt what we previously thought impossible. He presses us into challenges that demand far greater power from Him than we've ever known. He shows us a life we've never dreamed we could live.

It is for this other Jesus that people inside and outside the church are searching today. We are like sailboats tossing in a restless sea, waiting for a stiff, bracing wind to fill our sails and get us moving according to the Master's charts and toward His goals.

Sometimes the other Jesus speaks hard words to wake us up. He takes our breath away with His soul-sized challenges and with His offer to accomplish them through us. The "hard sayings" of Jesus confront us with the other half of the Gospel—the alarming, amazing, and awesome potential entrusted to us as followers of Christ. These are the sayings of the Master we often skim over or avoid in our search for teachings that appeal to us.

Some are hard in that they are difficult to understand at

first glance. They cause us to say, "I wonder what Jesus really meant by that." Often we pass over them, muttering, "Well, someday I hope I can understand what that means; it's beyond me now!" These hard sayings are like hidden treasures available to us only if we are willing to dig out their true meaning with the Master's help. Others are like islands: we must row around them until we discover where to land and how to establish a beachhead of deeper understanding.

Still others are hard sayings because they are difficult to live. We exclaim, "Who could ever live that way? The challenge is beyond me!" That's exactly the reaction the other Jesus wants. "Of course you can't live out my challenges on your own," He says to us. "I never meant for you to try without My power. Living in you, I will give you the strength and courage." When we hear that, we discover that the training manual of authentic Christ-empowered discipleship is given us in these hard sayings. And when we dare to live them with His power, we begin to know His mind, grow in His ways, and become more like Him. We move beyond the dull routines of traditional religion.

But there's a further reason some of Jesus' words are called hard sayings. They cut like a laser into the hard places in our hearts. These sayings cause an implosion in our inner being which results in an explosion of new priorities, values, and attitudes. We are forced to evaluate our prejudices and reactions. Our lives are turned upside-down—really right-side up—for the first time. The other Jesus blows the cap off our reservations. We discover a Lord who not only helps, but heals; who not only is sensitive to our cares, but enlists us in caring enough to serve. We are lifted out of the malaise of ambivalence into the resoluteness of decisive living.

Recently, I did a study of these hard sayings and rediscovered the other Jesus. From this study came this book—along with a renewed conviction that our lives and our spiritual growth depend on accepting the challenges Jesus gives us in these bracing, sometimes unsettling, hard sayings. They really offer the secret of how to put Him first in our lives and begin to live at full potential.

The Gospels and Revelation are filled with these hard sayings spoken by Jesus during His ministry and later as resurrected Lord to the churches of Asia Minor. Some biblical scholars have listed as many as one hundred and fifty of them; others underline around seventy.

I have selected fifteen of the hard sayings. They speak to our deepest needs today beneath our surface concerns and wants. Each of the following chapters will focus on one of these hard sayings specifically, and others that illuminate the meaning will be woven into the explanation. As we move through them, we will find hope to match our real needs.

Our lives—now and forever—depend on meeting the other Jesus!

CHAPTER TWO

Most assuredly, I say to you, unless you eat the flesh of the Son of Man and drink His blood, you have no life in you. Whoever eats My flesh and drinks My blood has eternal life, and I will raise him up at the last day. For My flesh is food indeed, and My blood is drink indeed. He who eats My flesh and drinks My blood abides in Me, and I in him.
(John 6:53-56)

THE STRUGGLE TO KEEP STRUGGLING

In introducing the other Jesus, I want to begin with the hard saying that prompted many of His followers to say, "This is a hard saying; who can understand it?" (John 6:60). Before looking at the hard saying they were reacting to, let's move into the story of what has just happened.

Jesus had performed the miracle of multiplying five barley loaves of bread and a few pieces of fish into enough food to feed five thousand people. His followers, who were part of the self-concerned, want-oriented generation of that time, were astounded. They, like so many contemporary Christians, were attracted to Jesus only for what He could do to meet their surface desires.

Later, when the crowds of these enthusiastic followers pursued Jesus around the Sea of Galilee to Capernaum, He confronted them with their limited expectations of what He could do for them. He told them that He wanted to satisfy a much deeper hunger and thirst inside them. Boldly, He claimed to be the bread of life. He told them that those who would come to Him would never hunger and that those who believed in Him would never thirst. Quite a promise!

Startled by the audacity of that promise, the people were further stunned by Jesus' claim to have come down from heaven. In amazement, the people said, "Is this not Jesus the son of Joseph, whose father and mother we know? How is it then that He says, 'I have come down from heaven'?" The question made way for Jesus' declaration of His ultimate purpose—to give the gift of eternal life.

No wonder the Jews quarreled among themselves over what Jesus meant. Their previous adulation turned to acrimony. I'm thankful they expressed their disdain. It brought forth one of the most hopeful of the hard sayings of the other Jesus: "Most assuredly, I say to you, unless you eat the flesh of the Son of Man and drink His blood, you have no life in you. Whoever eats My flesh and drinks My blood has eternal life, and I will raise him up at the last day. For My flesh is food indeed, and My blood is drink indeed. He who eats My flesh and drinks My blood abides in Me, and I in Him" (John 6:53–56).

The Meaning of the Metaphor

That did it! If the masses of would-be followers had been stunned and startled before, now they were shocked. I like the *New English Bible*'s translation of their reaction: "This is more than we can stomach! Why listen to such words?" (John 6:60).

We may have the same reaction. At first, this hard saying

may strike us as revolting, even nauseating, until we catch the inner meaning of Jesus' earthy Aramaic idiom.

We will begin to understand Jesus' words better when we compare them with some of the other visceral idioms of the time. In Jesus' day, when people had worked to the point of exhaustion, it was not unusual for them to say, "I have eaten my body and drunk my blood." In other words, they had given themselves completely to their task. Also, when a leader called for the unreserved commitment of his followers, he demanded that they eat his flesh and drink his blood. We see, then, that this was a colorful metaphor for total loyalty and allegiance.

And before we judge Jesus' hard saying as too crude, we need to reflect on some of our own everyday expressions in which we use words like "flesh," "blood," and "heart."

We talk about "sweating blood." Winston Churchill often is quoted in his appeal for commitment of "blood, sweat, and tears" in the dark days of World War II. We refer to demanding people as "bloodsuckers." When we think someone is expecting too much from us, we say, "What do you want, my life's blood?" Or in a moment of excelling, or getting something someone else has wanted, we say, "Eat your heart out, friend!"

We don't expect such statements to be taken literally, but they do express the close identification we make between our thinking and feeling and our physical life. And we'd all know what was meant if someone affirmed his or her support of us by expressing it in metaphor, "I'm for you with every fiber of my being."

The idea of eating Christ's flesh and drinking His blood may offend our sensibilities. But when we grapple with His true meaning, we see that what appears at first glance to be a brash suggestion of cannibalism is really an invitation to commitment, an introduction to profound communion, and an induction to a breathtaking commission. The other Jesus has unveiled an offer of a totally new quality of relationship with Him and a new sustenance to empower it.

Why, then, did Jesus' followers object so strongly to what they called a hard saying? It was hard not because they found it difficult to understand, but because they understood it all too well. He boldly called them to accept Him as God's Son and commit their lives to Him. For that, He promised them lasting satisfaction of their spiritual hungers and thirsts, and life after death. Wouldn't everyone want that? Perhaps not, if it required total commitment to the One who offered it. Jesus' followers, religious people who did not know God personally, resisted His impelling call to commit themselves to Him. Life was a struggle because of unmet spiritual needs. All He required was to accept Him as Lord of their lives. Could it be that they had become so accustomed to struggling that they could not believe that giving Jesus their undivided allegiance would make any difference?

The Habit of Struggling

I'm convinced that many of us struggle very hard to keep struggling. We have become so used to life's being a struggle that we struggle even with Jesus, who is the solution to overcoming our struggles.

What would you say is your biggest struggle? Recently, I asked my congregation and television viewers across the nation that question.

One man wrote a very startling reply. "Struggles? My whole life is a struggle! And why is that? I know that the solution to struggling is turning my life over to Christ. But there's someone who stands in the way, keeping me from doing that.

He tells me I will lose control and that it might not work anyway. Who is this person blocking me? It is I!"

I couldn't get that very honest reply off my mind as I read the thousands of other responses. A growing concern was confirmed. When I asked people to share their needs or problems, the same old frustrations surfaced. People are struggling today, and the same struggles keep recurring. Often I'm told about the same ones from the same people—year after year! Could it be that we have developed a false security in struggling?

This has led me to a disturbing conclusion about contemporary Christianity in America. Many Christians have become habitual strugglers. We struggle with life's pressures, with difficult people, and with challenges. We want Jesus' strength for these minor struggles, but we resist His solution to our biggest struggle.

That one great struggle that is going on inside most of us is the struggle to run our own lives. We don't have much difficulty accepting Jesus as our Savior, as One who forgives and comforts us. It's our struggle with His uncompromising call to make Him absolute Lord of our lives that causes us to continue to do battle with the anxieties of life. Committing our lives to Him as Lord is the secret of receiving His power for our daily problems and for our worry about death. All that He offers us for abundant living now and eternal life beyond the grave is available only when we surrender to His Lordship.

Without that unreserved surrender, we continue to live as spiritual paupers. It's as if we've been accustomed to not having adequate financial resources to meet our daily needs, but then are told we've been given a limitless inheritance to spend. We are astounded, but our habit patterns of worrying over making ends meet keep us from drawing on the inheritance.

Hetty Green is a classic example. When she died she left an estate valued at over one hundred million dollars. She denied herself any pleasures. Beyond that, she did not use any of her wealth to help others. Her life was a constant struggle. She ate cold oatmeal to save on fuel. Her house was never warm, and her appearance was shabby. When her son needed medical attention for a growth on his leg, she delayed while trying to find a free clinic. In fact, she delayed so long that her son's leg finally had to be amputated. Hetty lived like a pauper when she was wealthy.

Many of us live like that spiritually. We need more than a temporary tonic in trouble. Our greater need is to realize the spiritual inheritance that is ours if we will only commit our lives to Jesus. He is the all-powerful, reigning Lord. And obedience to Him as Lord is the key to the filling of the hunger and thirst inside us that keeps us struggling.

The Power That Breaks the Pattern

The level of commitment that gets us beyond the stage of constant struggle must be very specific. Many of us believe in Jesus, but have never prayed a prayer of commitment. The primary meaning of eating Christ's flesh and drinking His blood is that we become committed followers, turning over our minds, emotions, wills, and bodies for Jesus' absolute, unquestioned control. That surrender must then be followed by yielding the strategic areas of our lives—our relationships, our work, our money, and our plans and hopes for the future. After that we are ready to make an inventory of the struggles we are facing right now and entrust each one to Jesus for His guidance and intervening power.

Having made that kind of all-inclusive commitment, we are prepared to consider the second and deeper implication of Jesus' hard saying. To eat Christ's flesh and drink His blood means to accept what He has done for us. That assures us of never having to endure these struggles again.

Lasting Nourishment

Jesus calls us to eat of His flesh, the Bread of Life. The Hebrew word for "flesh," used throughout His message, meant humanity. When He referred to His own flesh, He was talking about His incarnation. We are to feed on the sublime fact that He, the Son of God, eternal Logos, God's ultimate Word about Himself and what He created us to be, "dwelt among us full of grace and truth." Feasting on that in the banquet halls of our minds satisfies our gnawing spiritual hunger. In wonderment, we contemplate what He did for us, "in the flesh." We never tire of chewing that over, thoroughly digesting its magnificent nourishment.

The bread Jesus offers us to eat is His life which He gave and gives for "the life of the world." Calvary! Christ, Immanuel, died for you and me. When I feed the hunger of my soul with that liberating, substitutionary sacrifice for my sins, I know what hunger pangs I never need experience again. I don't have to wonder about my status. I am loved, completely forgiven. I don't have to worry about my worth. Christ gave His body, His flesh, His life for me. And I don't have to be troubled by death or where I will spend eternity. When I eat of the fact and truth of the cross, I take into myself the assurance of eternal life and the confidence that I'm alive forever and heaven has begun for me. And that renewed realization forces me to exclaim, in the words of my own paraphrase of an anonymous poem,

> I constantly think about the cross
> And close my eyes to see

The cruel nail and crown of thorns
And Jesus crucified for me.
But even could I see Him die,
I could but see a little part
Of that great love which, like a fire,
Is always burning in His heart.

The more we think about that love, the more we are prompted to feed on its implications for us personally. Jesus not only died to give us eternal life, but to give us what we need for the daily, moment-by-moment experience of the abundant life—life to the fullest.

We all share a hunger to live to the full measure of Christ's potential for us in each of the remaining days we have on earth. And that's so much more than His help to get us through each day's challenges and troubles. We really "eat Christ's flesh" when we come to grips with His promise that the life He lived can be the quality of our new life in Him. We are called to love as He loved; forgive as He forgave; heal minds, bodies, and relationships as He healed; serve as sacrificially and unselfishly as He served. That too is part of the mysterious treasure of this hard saying. And it does collide with the hard place in us. Christ's bread is offered for discipleship. "Impossible!" we say. "How can we live like Jesus?"

Drinking Christ's Blood

The truth is, we can't and don't . . . unless we combine eating His flesh with drinking His blood. We wonder about that. We can appreciate why the followers of Jesus were astonished by that challenge, but we find it a hard idea to comprehend and appropriate today. They recoiled at the idea of drinking His blood. He stood before them with His lifeblood coursing in His veins. Christ is now our risen Lord. How can we drink the blood of one who is a Spirit? And what, exactly, do we drink when we drink Christ's blood today?

The Hebrew understanding of the blood was rooted in the conviction that blood in an animal or a person was the life. That dated back to Moses and the saying "The blood is the life" (Deut. 16:23). For us, to drink Christ's blood means to take His very life into us. He chose the metaphor to dramatize the meaning of dwelling in constant union with Him. His own words explain: "He who eats My flesh and drinks My blood abides in Me and I in him" (John 6:56).

The allegory of the vine and the branches communicates the same truth. "I am the vine, you are the branches. He who abides in Me, and I in him, bears much fruit; for without Me you can do nothing" (John 15:5). This is the mystical union of Christ in us—the dynamic power of Christ's Spirit for living the abundant life He promised. He says to us, "You must take My life inside you. I must live in your thinking brain, flow through your emotions, course through your physical body. My mind must become your mind, My will your will, My priorities your priorities, My strength your strength."

A Momentous Assurance

Now we see that this hard saying is really a momentous assurance. Jesus is not calling us only to emulate His example; He is inviting us to assimilate Him, His actual Spirit, His life. When we drink Him in, we absorb into ourselves His life, His teaching, His character, His ways, His virtue, His wisdom.

This is so much more than what has been lightly called "imitating Christ." It is possible to imitate what isn't a part of us. Seeking to do what Jesus did—or even to ask, "What would Jesus do?"—still is on the meager level of imitation where so many Christians today are trying to live with self-generated piety. That's not what Jesus offers. He seeks to give us the impelling inspiration of His indwelling Spirit. And this is no transitory experience, but permanent union. The words of what first sounded like a hard saying are really like the announcement of water to someone about to die of thirst, or food for someone who is starving.

Some Serious Questions

That prompts some questions I suspect have been forming in your mind. Why do we resist having our aching thirst for Christ's Spirit satisfied? Why do we try to live the Christian life on our own strength? Why are we satisfied with the life of trying so hard, experiencing ups and downs in our spiritual life?

Could it be that this saying is hard for us because we are afraid of losing our control and of what the indwelling Christ might want to do in us and through us? If it's true that He seeks to continue His ministry through us, and I am convinced He does, then we may be wondering what that will cost us.

During His ministry on earth as Jesus of Nazareth, caring for people cost Him His privacy. His life was spent for the needs of people. He served others rather than demanding that they serve His needs. He loved the unlovely and forgave those who, according to our standards, didn't deserve to be forgiven. He ministered to the sick and suffering; He touched lepers and befriended outcasts. Are we afraid he will instigate some of the same kind of ministry through us?

When we consider what drinking in Christ may mean, we can identify with the response of those who said, "This is a hard saying!" But the other Jesus did not change His offer by making it easier. The ranks of His followers thinned. Previously enraptured listeners turned away. Champions of His cause found other things demanding their time and attention. John records the stark reality of a dwindling movement. Such a report would put panic into the heart of a religious leader today as he counted his congregation or reviewed the Nielsen ratings of a shrinking viewer audience of his media ministry. "From that time many of His disciples went back and walked with Him no more" (John 6:66).

Is it any different today? Will we also balk at the high cost of eating Christ's flesh and drinking His blood? Is it too hard a saying for us? Can we throw caution to the wind, accept the full impact of His incarnation, and invite Him to live in us?

The other Jesus wants to know. He asks us what He asked the inner circle of His disciples. "Do you also want to go away?"

Quite honestly, sometimes we do. In times of selfishness and pride we'd like to run our own lives again. And at other times, when in reality we've left, abdicating active discipleship, we still are around in our churches acting like faithful disciples.

But deep inside all of us there's a person Jesus is counting on. Our true self. There in our inner being, we know the real issues. And with Simon Peter we are both shocked that the Lord had to ask and resolute in our renewed commitment in response. "Lord, to whom shall we go? You have the words of eternal life. Also, we have come to believe that You are the Christ, the Son of the living God" (John 6:68).

When we really believe that, we are ready to see how Jesus' hard saying gives us the secret of overcoming the struggle to grow in the Christian life. When we eat Christ's flesh and drink His blood, we actually receive His Spirit, and we begin to grow in what Paul called "the measure of the stature of the fullness of Christ" (Eph. 4:13).

The Fullness of Christ

The fullness of Christ includes His mind for our thoughts, His nature for the formation of our character, His person for the shaping of our personalities, His will for the direction of our wills, His power for our actions.

Once we have yielded our inner life to the formation of Christ in us, we can face the struggles of our outer life. Each new challenge or difficulty calls for greater inner growth in His fullness. Our first reaction will not be to cast about for direction or solutions in the circumstances, but to turn inward to Christ living in us. We can thank Him that out of the fullness of the wisdom, knowledge, and vision of His divine intelligence we will be guided in what to think and what to do. The otherwise disturbing pressures of life will become an opportunity for further formation of Christ's fullness in us. To a greater degree every day, we will think and react in oneness with Him.

Praying that Christ in His fullness be formed in us relieves us of three of the most troublesome struggles of life. The first is our struggle with our human nature. That struggle includes our thoughts, inner feelings, and selfishness. It's a wearying, grim battle to try to change ourselves. Resolutions, improvement programs, and self-discipline efforts yield little change in our basic nature. But when we honestly confess our defeat in trying to get better and we ask for the fullness of Christ, He enters in and performs a continuing miracle of making us like Himself.

Second, we are freed from the struggle to be adequate. I know I am insufficient for the demands of life, but I also know Christ is all-sufficient. I can't imagine any problem He can't solve, any person He could not love, or any challenge He would not be able to tackle. And so, from within me as well as around me, Christ is at work giving me what I could never produce without Him.

And third, we don't have to struggle with worries over what the future holds. We can be assured that what the Lord allows to happen will be used for greater growth of His fullness in us. We can relax. Whatever we face will be an opportunity for new dimensions of His character to be formed in us.

All this is based on a reverent conviction. Just as in the incarnation the Spirit of God was blended in perfect harmony with Jesus' human nature, so too, in a powerful way, His Spirit dwells in our humanness and He is formed in us. The more we yield our lives to Him, the more He forms us into His image. It is a lifelong process, and He's never finished with us.

Authentic Christians

The most exciting thing I am witnessing today is the authentic renewal of Christians. The other Jesus is raiding the ranks of the need-oriented, "me generation" of Christians who previously have been satisfied with a bland, anemic faith. The crucial difference is that those who have wanted Jesus for what He could do for their surface wants have been transformed by His indwelling Spirit and He is meeting their deeper hunger and thirst.

In a remarkable way, I see just the reverse of the response of the followers of Christ when He first spoke this hard saying. The ranks of traditional church people may be thinning in some churches and denominations, but not so for this new breed of contemporary, Spirit-filled disciples who have found that this hard saying is really a gracious promise of a new beginning.

Four Qualities of the Other Jesus Movement

This renewal has four crucial qualities, and they become an inventory for all of us. (1) The people who are taking Jesus seriously today have made a new commitment to live for Christ as the dynamic center of their lives. (2) They have invited His Spirit to live in them. (3) They feed on Him in consistent daily study of the Scriptures. The hard sayings have become their training manual for obedient discipleship. (4) And within them, the indwelling Lord is leading them into faithfulness in communicating His grace and serving Him in costly ways.

The other Jesus is on the move. He frees us from the need to struggle to keep struggling.

CHAPTER THREE

And no one, having drunk old wine, immediately desires new;
for he says, "The old is better."
(Luke 5:39)

OLD WINE IN NEW SKINS

My church in Hollywood is located on a busy street. To catch the attention of people going by, we have placed a large, prominent sign over the main entrance. It not only displays the name of the church, but it also announces each week the title of my forthcoming Sunday sermon.

One week the title of my sermon was the same as the title of this chapter, and it caused quite a stir. The secular crowd was amazed that I was going to talk about wine. Some Christians, however, who thought they knew their Bibles, were afraid that a mistake might have been made in the title. Many of them called the church to straighten me out. One of them was particularly happy to point out what he thought was a confusion in the wording.

"I've seen your sermon title morning and evening as I've

driven to and from work this week. I suspect you're going to be talking about the parable of wineskins. If that's the case, you've got the words all mixed up. It should be 'New Wine in Old Wineskins.' "

"That would be true," I said, "if I were focusing on the first part of the parable. The second part is about *old* wine in *new* skins."

"Is that in the Bible?" he challenged. "I've never seen that!"

"Sure is," I responded. "Check Luke 5:39. Jesus was as concerned about the problem of old wine in new skins as he was about new wine in old skins."

"Okay," the man replied, "but I'll be there Sunday with my Bible in hand just to check you out!"

My caller was faithful to both his promise and his challenge. He sat in the front row right below the pulpit with his open Bible in hand. I could tell that he was as surprised as some of my regular members to discover that in Luke's Gospel Jesus concluded his parable on the wineskins with a strange twist: "And no one, having drunk old wine, immediately desires new; for he says, 'The old is better' " (Luke 5:39).

You're probably wondering why I call that a hard saying. It sounds like a simple, flat-out statement about a wine connoisseur's preference for old wine. So what's so "hard" about Jesus' saying? At first it doesn't seem difficult either to understand or to accept. But when we understand the implication of what Jesus said here, we are convinced that it is indeed a hard saying.

Hearing on Three Levels

Before we can fully appreciate the meaning of these words, we need to hear them on three levels. To begin with, we must hear them through the ears of the people to whom Jesus was first speaking. Next, we must hear these words through the ears of the first-century inquirers of the Christian faith for whom Luke wrote. Finally, we must hear through our own ears that are attuned to a twentieth-century world. And we can catch the deeper meaning in all of these three levels of listening as we come to a fresh understanding of the parable of the wineskins itself. What prompted it? Why did Luke record it along with this concluding saying? And what does it mean to us today?

The Setting

The parable of the wineskins was given by Jesus in Capernaum in response to the scribes and Pharisees who were very critical of his non-conforming ministry. Just prior to recounting the parable itself (Luke 5:36–39), Luke records what Jesus said and did to disturb the religious leaders.

While He was preaching and teaching in a house there with the crowds pressing in around Him, four men tore open the roof and lowered down alongside Jesus a paralyzed man on a stretcher. They could not wait. They had to get their friend in touch with the Master. Imagine the consternation of the religious leaders over this interruption, especially when Jesus' response was not only to heal the man, but to tell him his sins were forgiven. Once again Jesus was accused of blasphemy. "Who can forgive sins but God alone?" murmured the outraged scribes and Pharisees.

The Other Jesus—A Friend of "Sinners"!

Next, we see Jesus walking along the street where He met Levi, a tax collector whose name was also Matthew. Tax collectors were abhorred conspirators with the Romans. They collected import and export taxes along the road running through Capernaum. Not only did they demand the tax for Antipas, but many of them gouged exorbitant taxes from their victims and pocketed any amount they could get above what they had to pay Antipas. The Jews hated the tax collectors and categorized them all as enemies. But Jesus saw Matthew as a man in need of love and forgiveness, not merely as a tax collector.

Now it was bad enough for Jesus to associate with Matthew at all, but next we see that He accepted an invitation to go to dinner at his house. He enjoyed a meal with Matthew's guests, some of whom were also tax collectors and others whom Jesus' enemies classified as outcasts and sinners.

And, as if that wasn't enough, the rage in the scribes and Pharisees was brought to a boiling point when they saw that Jesus' disciples didn't keep the regulation of fasting. A good Jew at that time was required to fast on Mondays and Thursdays. Few people knew why they were fasting, but they kept the rule out of a sense of religious duty.

Jesus responded to the criticism of His disciples by explaining that their life with Him as His disciples was like a marriage banquet. In those days a full week was spent with the bride and groom in the celebration of their marriage. And according to the rabbinical rule, during that week the bridal party and their friends were relieved of all religious observances like fasting.

Jesus asked, "Can you make the friends of the bridegroom fast while the bridegroom is with them? But the days will come when the bridegroom will be taken away from them; then they will fast . . ." (Luke 5:34–35). In saying this the Master clearly identified Himself as the bridegroom and insisted that life with Him was a joyous celebration. He also indicated that He understood what the scribes and Pharisees were plotting. He knew they wanted to do away with Him because of His disregard for their endless lists of regulations.

Tradition Threatened

It was the tradition of the officialdom that Jesus threatened. He was not opposed to the Law and to reverence for God. In fact, he constantly called people to put God first in their lives. But the scribes and Pharisees were not concerned with the man-made traditions built up over the years. They were committed to the past, and they resisted change.

Now we can appreciate the full impact of Jesus' parable of the patchcloth and wineskins and the saying about people's preference for old wine. "No one puts a piece from a new garment on an old one; otherwise the new makes a tear, and also the piece that was taken out of the new does not match the old. And no one puts new wine into old wineskins; or else the new wine will burst the wineskins and be spilled, and the wineskins will be ruined. But new wine must be put into new wineskins, and both are preserved. And no one, having drunk old wine, immediately desires new; for he says, 'The old is better' " (Luke 5:36–39).

The parable of the new patch introduces the point Jesus wants to make. His preaching of the kingdom of God, His gospel, His presence, and His joy are the new life He offers His followers. This new life is not simply a patch-up of the old, worn, threadbare cloth of the old traditions of the scribes and Pharisees. Jesus had not come as the Messiah, the Word of God, to repair and preserve customs and practices that were part of an external religion actually keeping people from fellowship with the Father. The parable is a warning. A patch from a new, unshrunk material would actually tear an old garment. More than that, it just would not match. The new life in Christ could not be used simply to preserve an old religious life of rules and regulations.

A Known to Teach an Unknown

Jesus then went on to drive home His point with a familiar metaphor. The parable of the wineskins utilized a truth about fermenting wine that all of His listeners were aware of. Note how Jesus takes a known to teach an unknown; He uses what they already understand to communicate what they urgently need to understand.

The disciples and the scribes and Pharisees understood the danger of putting new wine into old wineskins. In Jesus' day, wine was fermented in the skins of goats. After the flesh, bones, and insides of the goat had been removed, the skin was tanned over fires of acacia wood. Then the openings were securely sewn. The neck of the skin became the spout for pouring in the unfermented grape juices. When the skin was full, the neck was sutured tightly, and the turbulent fermentation process began.

When it was finished, the new wineskin was stretched to full capacity. Once the wine was used, the empty skin was dried. As it hardened, it became inflexible, and most of all, incapable of further elasticity. It could be used for water, but it could no longer be used as a wineskin, for the fermentation process would burst the skin and both the wine and the skin would be lost.

The Meaning of the Metaphors

We need to be sure we understand Jesus' metaphors. The new wine represented His new teaching of the kingdom of

God. Through Luke's eyes, it also meant Jesus' promise of abiding in His followers and the fulfillment of that promise at Pentecost. For us, the new wine is nothing less than Jesus Himself, Lord of our lives and indwelling Spirit.

But let's be very clear about the wineskins. To be sure, Jesus meant them to represent Israel as the people of God, but He also meant that each of the people who first heard the parable were intended to be a wineskin to contain the dynamic, fermentive, life-changing power of His gospel.

Nothing less is expected of us. We are to be new wineskins distinguished for our elasticity, flexibility, and adjustability as containers of not only Jesus' revolutionary teaching, but His own indwelling presence. I like to think of our minds, emotions, and wills as the wineskins of Christ's new wine today.

A Difficult Question

When we try to apply that privilege to our own experience, a question focuses in our minds. The parable does not answer the question directly. If a wineskin can be used only once for the fermenting of wine, how does the parable explain our need for daily renewal through fresh infillings of Christ's Spirit? The implication is that we are to present Christ with a new wineskin of an open mind, a receptive heart, and a ready will that is anxious to obey His guidance. That must be done every day.

The challenge is not as simple as it sounds. Like the scribes and Pharisees, we become secure in our own traditions and resist change. We become satisfied with what we've experienced of the Lord's power in our lives and are fearful of new challenges. Our wineskin becomes dry, brittle, and inflexible as we fearfully try to maintain the status quo of our life in Christ.

The Hard Saying

Now we can see why Jesus' conclusion to the parable of the new wine and new wineskins is a hard saying. We say about the wine of our stage of growth in Christ, "The old is better." We feel comfortable with words like "Give me the oldtime religion—it's good enough for me." But what we really mean is "Allow me to stay where I am. I know all I need to know. I am content with what I have and what I have experienced."

There is a kind of Christianized pharisaism that can so easily attack us. I think that's why Luke included this hard saying in his Gospel. In his missionary ventures with the Apostle Paul, Luke had ample opportunity to witness at first hand the early Christians who resisted personal growth in Christ and blocked the expansion of Christianity to the gentile world. Luke was very familiar with those who wanted to keep Christianity as a sect of Judaism and who insisted that converts to Christ first had to become full-fledged Jews before becoming part of the church. Equally disturbing were those quickly born Christians who slipped back into their old personality traits and thought patterns instead of moving on in courageous discipleship. Luke, of all the Gospel writers, felt the importance of including this hard saying not just to explain the traditionalism in the Pharisees of Jesus' day, but also in first-century Christians who had become old wineskins.

The same can be true of us in these last years of the twentieth century. We too can become content with the vintage wine of our comfortable ideas, settled attitudes, and self-satisfied complacency.

Old Wine in New Skins

But there's an even deeper problem for most of us—old wine in new skins. We pray daily for the Lord's will in our lives, and in our worship we sing hymns of commitment. Some of us are part of renewal movements in which we seek new power for ourselves and the church, and yet many would have to say honestly that they have not received new spiritual power to face life's difficult people and soul-stretching problems. After all the singing, preaching, study group interaction, prayer, and fellowship is over, we don't feel or act like Spirit-filled and empowered people. Why?

I think it is because we offer the Lord a new wineskin, but we want to fill it with *old* wine. And what does old wine do in a new wineskin? It just sits there!

I meet Christians all over the world who are trying to be new wineskins but are satisfied with the old wine of what they have known and experienced in the past. The other day I had a visit with a well-known Pentecostal leader. He said, "It's a challenge to help people who have been part of a denomination committed to renewal to remain open to the fresh infilling of the Lord's Spirit. Some of our people become so proud of their initial baptism of the Spirit and our familiar brand of church life and worship, it is truly difficult to help them experience the new wisdom and power the Lord wants to give each day. Renewing a renewalist and enabling a fresh Pentecost for Pentecostals is a challenge!"

The same thing can happen to many of us who have settled into old patterns. Cherishing our theology of clique words and slick phrases, we constantly rehearse what happened to us some time ago rather than rejoice in what the Lord is doing in us now. The problem is intensified when we find other people whose experience and language matches ours.

We join with them and become an "Old Wine Society."

Just the opposite is happening to people in our church in Hollywood. I'm so thankful for the many Elders who not only present Christ with a new wineskin each day, but also have a thirst for His new wine. That's not always easy for a church with a great heritage of renewal and worldwide leadership in the evangelical movement. Our traditions, plus the memories of past glory, could easily keep us from the new power the Lord is ready to pour out today. We are discovering that the church must constantly be a new wineskin ready for the dynamic power of the new wine of the Lord's fresh strategies in evangelism, program, and worship. Only new wineskins filled with new wine can handle that challenge.

Brad's Story

My friend Brad is an example of a new wineskin filled with new wine. He's a busy movie producer, but his primary commitment is to Christ and his calling to be an Elder in the church. The other day at lunch, Brad shared with me an exciting thing that was happening in his life. He told me that a few months ago he had said to himself, "If Christ is who He says He is, the reigning Lord of all and the source of power and joy, then I'm either stupid or insane if I don't spend a period of time with Him in prayer and reading the Bible each morning."

Brad made a commitment to get up an hour early every morning for a quiet time with the Lord. He could hardly contain his joy and enthusiasm as he told me about the profound insight, stimulating vision, and specific guidance these times alone with the Lord were providing him. Brad is giving the Lord a fresh wineskin each day and is being filled with new wine. The result has been personal growth and a desire for the Lord's best for the church. As an Elder thirsty for new wine, he is a channel through which the Lord's new direction for the church as a whole is flowing.

A New Wine Society

What's happening to Brad is also happening to the professional staff and so many of the other Elders of our church. On Sunday mornings we meet before the first service, and their "Lord, we're ready for anything" spirit spurs me on as we pray together seeking to be new wineskins for the new wine the Lord has prepared for us and the church. Then when the pastors go into the chancel, the Elders enter the sanctuary as a group. They line up along the chancel steps. After the call to worship, and during the organ prelude, the pastors kneel behind the communion table and the Elders on the chancel steps.

Members and visitors in the pews tell me this expression of openness to what the Lord is going to say and do in the worship service raises their own expectancy level. At the end of the service the same Elders are available to pray with the many people who respond to the invitation to come forward to receive Christ or for prayers of healing for the spiritual, emotional, relational, and physical needs in their lives.

The significant thing to me is the way this healing ministry has evolved and is constantly being improved both in procedures and depth of understanding. We're learning how to pray for people and their manifold needs. And we never can be satisfied with whatever the Lord did on a previous Sunday. We've learned that each Sunday requires a new wineskin: for me as I preach, for the pastoral team in the leadership of different and innovative orders of worship each Sunday, and for the Elders as channels of prayer power. It would be dangerous to pray to be new wineskins and be satisfied with last week's, or even yesterday's, old wine.

New Wine for Every Member

That's no less true for every member of a church. In every congregation there are those who have not met Christ personally and who need to take the first step. But to get off on the right foot, they need to hear the challenging good news that being a Christian is being a new wineskin to receive the new wine of Christ's Spirit. And those who have been Christians and church members for years need to be reminded that they have been elected, called, and appointed to be new wineskins every day. Some may have become old wineskins filled with old wine. Others may pray to be new wineskins but are still trying to age the old wine of their commitment years ago or to preserve the limited knowledge of Jesus they have already attained.

A New Wineskin Every Day

Honesty would impel all of us to admit that there are times when we join the chorus singing the refrain, "The old is better!" That's understandable. Offering the Lord a new wineskin each day and being ready to receive the wine of His Spirit can be very demanding. We know that His fermentive power will press us to change our thinking, our personality, and anything else that might be making us ineffective as communicators of His life to others. We suspect He will call us to challenges beyond our ability. Any of us who keep a tight check on what we are willing to give of ourselves find that very threatening.

The reason we cherish the old wine is that we are afraid

of the new and of the changes it might require. So often we say, or project the impression of saying, "Well, that's who I am. Don't expect me to change. That's my nature. That's the way I've always been and you've just got to accept me the way I am!" And some of us who talk the loudest about our freedom to change may be advertising our weakness— we may be the least willing to have Christ tamper with our lives. We become not only content with ourselves, but actually defensive.

Only Christ Himself can break that pattern. And He does it by revealing to us the joy of being new wineskins and being filled with His new wine each day. Sometimes He gets through to us in perplexing problems that force us to see ourselves as we are. And often He creates a thirst for His new wine by showing us what He is doing in other people who have discovered the exhilarating adventure of offering themselves to Him as new wineskins. However, His most effective method is to continue to give us abundant grace and the faith to appropriate that grace.

That's the way it has been for me. I can remember the time that He gave me a thirst for new wine. After creating a dissatisfaction with the person I'd been, He led me to two verses. The first was a description of the abundance He wanted to give me and the second a promise of what I needed in order to receive the gift. John 1:16 caught my attention. "And of His fullness we have received grace for grace." I pondered what that meant.

"Grace for grace." A never-ending succession of experiences of unqualified love. The Lord had been very gracious to me, but I realized that I had become focused on previous outpourings of grace and was not living expectantly. So I prayed a very specific prayer: "Lord Jesus, I look forward to receiving your fresh grace in the challenges and difficulties of this day."

Then the "grace for grace" superabundance led me to another verse that promises a multiplied blessing. In Romans 1:17, Paul uses the phrase "from faith to faith." Again I asked for insight, and it struck me that in addition to the primary gift of faith to accept Christ as my Savior and Lord, He wanted to give me confident trust in Him in specifics.

As He guided me to anticipate new grace in the concerns ahead of me, He also gave me boldness to claim His power to do what I never would have attempted alone. That cured my desire to cherish old wine. I longed for the new wine as I began each day.

The needs of people around us also create a desire for new wine. When we begin the day offering the Lord a new wineskin of willingness and He fills us with His fullness, He gives us opportunities to share the enthusiasm of the zest and joy of the gift of grace and faith He has given us. We are led to people who need hope and encouragement. We become initiators in healing broken relationships. When others around us are in panic, we are confident that the Lord is in charge and will bring good out of the most grim circumstances. With the fresh morning draught of new wine invigorating us, the day will be filled with serendipities in which we can pour out what we have received. When we stop the inflow of fresh wine, the serendipities stop happening!

Flexible for the Future

Being the new wineskin filled with new wine gives us a totally different attitude toward the future. The Lord makes us flexible and open to new ways of doing old things. No longer committed to sameness, we become receptive to His unlimited creativity. We discover that there are no unsolvable problems but only opportunities masquerading as difficulties.

Instead of being problem people, with the Lord's wisdom and innovation we become problem-solvers.

Christ's hard saying penetrates to any hardness in us that resists change or is satisfied with what we have discovered of His grace thus far. We begin to be aware of how routine life can become. Our commitment to our religious traditions is exposed. We are alarmed that we may be holding up the Lord's progress in our churches by cherishing old customs and familiar ways of worship and program.

How can we know we are closed to the fresh new wine of the other Jesus? If we didn't begin today by offering the Lord a new, open, receptive, elastic wineskin, then it's our first day of knowingly cherishing the old wine of the present. . . . If we no longer expect surprises of grace to happen in each new day, we are on the way to a dull life. . . . If we have not received a new thought about the Lord and His magnificence, we are denying ourselves the intellectual growth He wants for us. . . . If we find ourselves longing for the "good old days," we will miss the great new days the Lord has planned. . . . If we say, "I never did it that way before," we are beginning to dig a rut of routine.

A New Beginning

Sandra, a woman in my congregation, has taken the other Jesus very seriously. Her prayer each morning is: "It's a new day. I'm a new wineskin open to the new wine of the kingdom, to Christ, His grace, faith to trust Him, and joy to share. I will think magnificently of Him today and be open to attempt things I've never tried before. I will share the new wine with my husband, family, friends, and anyone the Lord arranges for me to listen to and to love. I am willing to be different so that I can do old duties differently. Today is all I have.

Yesterday is past. I will not be satisfied with yesterday's discoveries or nurse false guilt over its failures. Today is the never-to-be-repeated gift of the Lord. He has made me ready for anything. And tomorrow? Not to worry. Like today, it's a new wineskin, new wine, a new beginning, a new life!"

We are all new wineskins by Christ's call and appointment to be His disciples. Now the only question is: Are we filled with old wine or new?

CHAPTER FOUR

It is easier for a camel to go through the eye of a needle than for a rich man to enter the kingdom of God.
(Mark 10:25)

CAUGHT IN THE EYE OF THE NEEDLE

I have a friend who is a "Monday morning quarterback" sermon analyst. "Great sermon yesterday," he said to me recently. "Exactly what those people need to hear!"

How I wish he'd said, "I really needed that message. I talk a better game than I live. I felt you knew my need and were preaching that message just for me!"

Instead, my friend was convinced that the sermon was for everyone else except him.

But before we become too critical of this seemingly self-satisfied analyst of other people's needs, let's reflect on the times when we may have reacted the way he did. Have you ever sidestepped a challenge because you felt it didn't apply to you? Have you ever felt a glow of superiority when others were discussing some problem you thought you'd conquered long ago or never faced?

Our reaction to some of the hard sayings of the other Jesus is like that. We assume they are for other people. And of all the hard sayings we are tempted to think do not apply to us, the one we most quickly dismiss is the one about the difficulty of a rich man's getting into the kingdom of God. Remember what Jesus said about the rich young ruler? "It is easier for a camel to go through the eye of a needle than for a rich man to enter the kingdom of God" (Mark 10:25).

How do you respond to that? Perhaps you expressed a sigh of relief, thinking, "Well, here's a hard saying that's not for me. I may have lots of problems, but having riches is not one of them!"

Strange thing. Being rich is a status we think belongs to someone else. And it's not just the disadvantaged who think of others as rich. Those who may have been able to achieve some measure of financial security usually do not think of themselves as rich. Even the wealthy refer to people who have more than they have acquired as "the rich." I can't remember having met anyone who touted the fact that he was rich and had all he wanted. And I have encountered only a very few people who would turn down the opportunity of being what they consider rich.

Whatever our monetary status, we all like money and the things it can buy. Our possessions are very important to us. They become a congealed extension of ourselves. And whether we worry about keeping what we have or getting more, our possessions can take possession of us.

This hard saying of Jesus is for all of us. Our preoccupation with material things gives us the rich man's problem even though we may not have his level of prosperity. We all run the danger of getting caught in the eye of the needle.

How we react to the challenge the other Jesus gave to the rich young ruler is a good test of the severity of our own problem: "One thing you lack: go your way, sell whatever you have and give to the poor, and you will have treasure in heaven; and come, take up your cross, and follow Me" (Mark 10:21). Mark then goes on to tell us that the rich young man was sad when he heard Jesus' words and went away grieved because he had great possessions.

Getting into the Story

Let's consider: What *would* you have done if Jesus were to put a challenge like that to you? And before my question makes me sound like the piously superior sermon critic I mentioned at the opening of this chapter, I must admit that Jesus' likening of the camel's difficulty in going through the eye of the needle to that of the rich young ruler in entering the kingdom is very disquieting to me. Like you, I'm unsettled by the "either-or" tone of Jesus' words. We've all grown much more comfortable with the "both-and" of believing in Jesus and keeping our own control of our possessions intact.

That's why the particular event is really our story. It's the biography of the contemporary Christian caught in the eye of the needle. True, Jesus' hard saying is hyperbole, that is, an exaggeration to make a point. But that point is sharp, and it easily penetrates our evaluation of what's important to us. To understand this hard saying better, let's take a closer look at the young man's strengths and also his needs.

There are so many laudable things about the rich young ruler with which we can empathize unashamedly. Like him, we all feel a deep spiritual hunger. However little or much material success we've attained, our inner emptiness brings us to the edge of the crowd along with the rich young man. With him, we are attracted to Jesus and His message about abundant and eternal life. We are magnetically drawn to His love, joy, and peace. His words of forgiveness and the opportunity to begin a new life captivate us. We are under the spell of the Master.

Meeting the Master

For the moment, we push aside our questions about the cost of discipleship, as did the rich young man. Our only concern is to meet the Master face to face. We want to know Him personally and feel the assurance of friendship with Him.

For the rich young ruler that moment came when he could no longer be satisfied with standing at the edge of the crowd listening and observing Jesus. As the Master left the crowd and started down the road, the young man was impelled by an inner, mysterious desire to run after Him. As he reached Jesus and met Him eye to eye, a strange mixture of admiration and awe gripped him, and he fell on his knees before the Master. Then, composing himself a bit, he got up and blurted out a question he must have rehearsed for days. "Good Teacher, what shall I do that I may inherit eternal life?"

We can feel both the urgency and the content of his question. We've all asked it. It's the question we ask when we want to know what's required of us to become a Christian. And it's what we keep on asking as we grow in the Christian life. What do I have to do? What must I attain? What are the qualifications of receiving and growing in a relationship with Christ?

A Profound Reply to an Urgent Question

For the rich young man, no other question could more clearly have exposed his spiritual problem. The one brief query revealed his confused thinking and his self-confidence. His careful salutation, "Good Teacher," betrayed his assumption that human goodness and the quality of life he had heard Jesus talking about were one and the same. He recognized that Jesus was "good." Clearly, he also thought of himself as a good man, and so he wanted to know what additional good thing he needed to do to add eternal life to his accumulated possessions. The man's use of the word "inherit" shows the extent to which he was hung up on this idea. An inheritance is something we claim as our right. We deserve it, we think. And the young man felt that some additional act of goodness would prove how deserving he really was.

Jesus' response was profound. "Why do you call me good? No one is good but One, that is, God." It was as if He said, "Do you call me good because you have accepted my claim to have come from God, who alone is good and the source of all goodness, or because you relate to me as just another rabbi in whom you see a human goodness you think you can attain by your own effort?"

However we interpret Jesus' initial response, it is obvious He saw that the young man overestimated his own ability to do something to win eternal life. To help him realize that his self-generated goodness was beyond his performance, Jesus reminded him of the second half of the Decalogue, enumerating the six moral implications of obedience to God: "Do not commit adultery; do not murder; do not steal; do not bear false witness; do not defraud; honor your father and your mother."

How very gracious of Jesus! He knew that the man's real problem was with the first commandment, "You shall have no other gods before me." With divine insight, Jesus knew that the man's possessions and his assumption of being a good man were standing in his way. When he naïvely asserted that he had impeccably fulfilled the commandments since his youth, Jesus simply caught his eyes and held his gaze intensely with "Oh, really?" accountability. Mark tells us, "Then Jesus, looking at him, loved him."

The Price of Real Treasure

Here we see the other Jesus in action. Motivated by profound love, He challenged the young man to do the one thing that would expose him to himself. Putting His finger on the raw nerve He had seen inside the man, He said in essence, "One thing you lack: go liquidate your assets so you are not tied to any thing or any place. Give to the poor from the abundance of that liquidation. Then you'll realize your true treasure in heaven. And you'll be free to take up a cross of absolute obedience to Me. If you can do this—then come and be one of My inner circle of disciples."

Again we wonder how we would have reacted. Or, more important, how are we responding right now? Our spiritual needs have brought us to Jesus. Face to face with Him, we feel the cost of discipleship to be exorbitantly high. The words "one thing you lack" reverberate in our minds. The word for "lack" in the Greek text is a form of the verb *husterō*, meaning "to be late, to come short, or to fail." Could our lack also be that we are more committed to our possessions than to Him?

We should note here that Jesus' challenge to the rich young ruler does not say that he was to give all of his liquidated assets to the poor. Rather, he was to get free from the tyranny of possessions over his soul. Then, once liberated, the young man was to use his means to care for the disadvantaged. It is significant, I believe, that Jesus did not make the "sell all" demand of Peter, James, and John. They were asked to leave their fishing business and become fishers of men. Mary and

Martha were not required to sell their house in Bethany. Nicodemus, also a ruler and probably rich, was not asked to sell his possessions as part of being "born again." But Jesus placed this condition on the rich young ruler because his treasuring of his treasures was keeping him from realizing his treasure in heaven.

The Greek word for treasure that Jesus used here, *thesauros*, refers to a container of riches or precious jewels. Jesus frequently spoke of the heart as the container or treasure chest of spiritual riches.

I've often wondered if the promise of treasure in heaven Jesus offered to the rich young ruler was something much more than life in heaven after death. The more I reflect on it, the more I'm convinced that Jesus was offering him the awesome opportunity right then, here on earth, of being a treasure chest of God in whom would be deposited the spiritual wealth of abundant living now as well as eternal life forever. There is no material treasure to be compared with that! When we realize that our lust for material things will rob us of that, we become alarmed. We begin to wonder what has filled the treasure chest of our own hearts. Are we adopting our culture's preoccupation with the accumulation of things and letting it stuff our hearts? These questions intensify our interest in what happened to the rich young ruler.

We see now that the young man was forced to make a decision. Mark describes his heartbreaking response. "He was sad at this word, and went away grieved, for he had great possessions" (Mark 10:22). The word "grieved" in the Greek conveys mental pain. Visualize the storm of conflict Jesus' challenge had caused in his mind and heart. The lightning of His call to discipleship was followed by loud claps of thunder that rumbled in the man's inner being and moved him to make his choice. His possessions were more important than the joy of eternal life, the delight of being treasured by God, and the adventure of being one of Jesus' intimate disciples. For the young man, his possessions were inseparable from the person he had become. He could not imagine life without them. They were more than his security; *they were his life*.

The rich young ruler was not the only one who felt grief that day. Even greater was the grief that Jesus felt as the young man walked away downcast and dejected. I imagine that the Master stood watching him, aching for him, as he disappeared from sight. It is very significant that Jesus didn't run after the young man and offer to change the terms of discipleship. That too is part of the character of the other Jesus. His love is unqualified and His offer of new life is unreserved, but He will not accommodate our secondary loyalties by changing His demand for our absolute commitment. We have a choice. And that's awesome . . . frightening!

The Eye of the Needle

When the young man was completely out of sight, Jesus turned to His disciples and said, "How hard it is for those who have riches to enter the kingdom of God!" He repeated the bold declaration of truth for emphasis. The second time, He clarified the deeper issue. "Children, how hard it is for those who trust in riches to enter the kingdom of God!" Then he went on to speak the hard saying we are considering in this chapter. "It is easier for a camel to go through the eye of a needle than for a rich man to enter the kingdom of God."

At first, the absurdity of these words makes us laugh. Then we realize that we may be laughing at ourselves, and suddenly our laughter sticks like a bone in our throats.

Jesus used the largest animal in Palestine and the smallest hole imaginable to stress a human impossibility. Some have suggested that He really meant a rope instead of a camel. They reason that when Jesus' Aramaic words in this hard saying were recorded in Greek, the similarity of the Greek word for camel, *kamelos*, and the word for a thick anchor rope, *kamilos*, caused them to be confused. Others have suggested that Jesus was referring to a small gate in Jerusalem which, in that day, was called "the eye of the needle." It was so small that when a camel tried to get through with cargo on its back, it would have to be unloaded and forced to its knees to make it through the small opening. But neither of these interpretations of Jesus' original hard saying changes the essential point: it is difficult for a person who trusts in riches to enter the kingdom of God.

Through the years, our understanding of this hard saying has been hampered by explanations that have altered the Master's original intent. Some have reasoned that the "one thing you lack" spoken to the rich young ruler can be applied to whatever it is that stands in our way of absolute obedience to Christ. Extensive lists of impediments have been proposed. The idea has been suggested, "Riches are probably not your concern, so just substitute whatever it is that might be holding you back in following Christ." That's a welcome relief for many who find that Jesus' reference to riches make them very uncomfortable. And as I mentioned earlier, since no one puts himself or herself into the category of being rich, Jesus' hard saying is usually dismissed as irrelevant to our spiritual needs. We miss the crucial message that our possessions can become camel-sized obstructions to entering and living in the kingdom of God.

The Issue of the Kingdom

We need to remind ourselves that the kingdom of God refers to His reign and rule over everything—our relationships, our responsibilities, and all of life, including our possessions. All that we have and are belongs to the Lord. And like the rich young ruler, what we have received as a gift can keep us from meeting, knowing, and enjoying the Giver. Or, what's worse, we can try to manipulate the Lord to keep a steady flow not only of the necessities of life, but of the luxuries we want.

The issue of entering the kingdom involves accepting Christ not only as our Savior, but also as our Lord. And that's the disturbing difficulty of most Christians today. We want Christ's love and forgiveness and assurance of life beyond the grave, but we find trusting Him in *all* of life is much more demanding.

Jesus insists on being Lord of all or not at all. And if we draw our security and sense of significance from our possessions, we have filled the "Lordship void" in all of us with things and not with Christ, and we are still caught in the eye of the needle. Not only does that rob us of the joy of discipleship now, but it would make us very uncomfortable in heaven. When the things we can't take with us become more important than the one thing we will take—our souls— then our eternal life is in jeopardy.

We count on our belief in Christ as Savior to assure us of heaven while we run our own lives now. But Christ calls us to make Him our Savior and our Lord. And making Him absolute Lord of our lives is the only way to make it through the eye of the needle.

Next, I am sure that we can identify with the reaction of the disciples. As they reflected on Jesus' hard saying, they asked, "Who then can be saved?" Their question tells us they still held the old idea that material wealth, along with protection from danger, was a sign of the blessing of God, of salvation. What they really were asking was, "If this man, so obviously blessed by God, can't be saved, who can?" We find ourselves in the same quandary at times. We wonder, "If God is the source of all of life's blessings, why would He allow a person to acquire so much material success and then not give him salvation, the greatest gift of all?" We often miss the same point the disciples missed: we fail to see that we may claim the blessings of God as our achievement and actually make them a substitute for Him. We treat Him as an addendum to what we have already determined are the values and goals of our lives. Again we say with the disciples, "Who then can be saved?"

Before Jesus responded to the disciples' question, I believe He must have looked at them intensely with eyes of love and patience. When He had their full attention, He spoke one of the most hopeful and encouraging truths He ever uttered: "With men it is impossible, but not with God; for with God all things are possible" (Mark 10:27). His words applied directly to the rich young ruler and have immense implications for all of us today.

Nothing Is Impossible for God

The rich young ruler was not an impossibility for God. Even his refusal of Jesus' call to discipleship that day did not write the last chapter of his spiritual life. The Lord was not finished with him.

What Jesus seems to be saying is that it is hard for a rich man to enter the kingdom, but not impossible, because God can do all things.

I think Jesus was looking forward to the time when He would suffer and die for the sins of the world. He would go to Calvary for the rich young ruler. And then, as risen, reigning Lord, He would continue to work on the minds and hearts of even the most resistant. The cross would be an even greater magnet of love than His ministry as Jesus of Nazareth. His Spirit would penetrate barriers, engender the gift of faith, and open people to His indwelling power. He would win out over the false gods of possessions.

In a sense, in His death and resurrection He would go through the eye of the needle for us. He would open the way for all to pass through who claim Him as Savior and Lord. And in the place of security in material riches He would give us the riches of His grace.

Paul captured the wonder: "For you know the grace of our Lord Jesus Christ, that though He was rich, yet for our sakes He became poor, that through His poverty, we might become rich" (2 Cor. 8:9). When we experience that spiritual wealth of grace, it becomes possible for us to put material wealth into proper prospective.

That's the vibrant hope in Jesus' statement that nothing is impossible for God. Looking into the future with complete trust, He could let the rich young ruler turn away because He knew that no refusal was final until the point of physical death. Jesus trusted God to do the impossible—to redeem the young man through the salvation His death and resurrection would make possible.

Many speculate, as I do, that the tight grip of the rich young man's possessions was broken and that he became a follower of Christ and a participant in the church after the resurrection. Some suggest that the account of the young man was Mark's own autobiography. Others think the young man was Barnabas, who, as a part of the church, sold all his possessions and laid the proceeds at the apostles' feet for the church's ministry to the poor. Those possibilities are more than a wishful desire for an "all's well that ends well" happy ending to the rich young ruler's story. As the early church expanded, the risen Lord did in fact win the absolute loyalty and unreserved commitment of many among the rich and powerful as well as the poor. Perhaps the rich young ruler was among them. It's not important to know, but what is crucial is how we respond to Jesus' conscripting call today.

When the Other Jesus Confronts Us

What if Jesus came to us today, met us face to face, and said, "One thing you lack. Liquidate your assets, give to the poor, claim that you are my treasure chest to receive my Spirit, take up your cross of obedience and follow me!"? "That's impossible!" we'd say. And so it is, on our own strength. But it wouldn't be for Immanuel, God with us. And the only response He wants from us is willingness.

The quality the other Jesus wants to give us is expressed in His first beatitude: "Blessed are the poor in spirit, for theirs is the kingdom of heaven" (Matt. 5:3). The truly blessed and happy people are those who can admit their spiritual need regardless of how much or little they have of material possessions. That sense of need is a gift of the Spirit of the other Jesus who persists until we are willing to put Him and the kingdom of God first. And what He does to get us through the eye of the needle and into the kingdom of His Lordship He continues to do to keep us from putting ourselves back into the eye again. The battle with possession by possessions is a lifelong struggle.

A man who had come through a financial crisis in which he had become a Christian said a remarkable thing. "Lloyd, living on the edge of financial need made me realize the spiritual emptiness of my life. I cried out to the Lord and He helped me through a terrible crisis. But now that things are going well for me, in fact, better than I ever imagined possible, I find it awfully difficult to pray with the same urgency.

Strange—the very help the Lord gave me has lessened my burning desire to know and serve Him. I'm really embarrassed by my seeming lack of gratitude, but on a daily basis I don't think as much about the Lord as I did when I was down and out. Now I guess I'm up and still out." That man is caught in the eye of the needle!

We all can empathize with him. Financial problems make us acutely aware of our spiritual needs. But when the Lord helps us climb out of the hole, we find it harder to trust Him completely. Having money and the things it can buy can quickly fill our sense of emptiness—for awhile, at least.

Money gives us a false sense of power. It gives us the ability to take care of the necessities of food, clothing, and housing. Money also makes us think we are free. With it we have the liberty to do what we want—travel, take vacations, indulge our hobbies, as well as collect the outward signs of success. And when we have a good balance in the bank and some fine stocks in our portfolio, we are tempted to feel we are finally free of financial concerns.

Then, too, we've learned that money talks. Indeed it does. Our deference to people who have financial power exposes our own sense of values and priorities. Often we cater to people who have inherited wealth or look admiringly at those who have worked hard, saved, invested wisely, and have multiplied their money. In financing spiritual, benevolent, or cultural causes, we tend to think of these people as categories on a major donor list rather than people who may have deep spiritual needs. Sometimes, pastors who talk about the sin of too much money are more than ready to give attention and admiration to people of wealth to assure the steady flow of their large contributions. They can be caught in the eye of the needle as much as the people they should be helping.

All of us, however much we have or hope to have, wrestle

with Jesus' hard saying. What shall we do with the other
Jesus who unsettles our materialism and our false security
of things? There are four crucial things this hard saying demands of us.

Four Crucial Demands

First, it challenges us to take Jesus seriously. His exaggeration in the hyperbole is to alarm us to the great danger of
making our possessions our false god. That forces us to ask,
"Have my possessions or desire for more of them caused me
to put second His absolute reign and rule over my life?"

Second, this hard saying measures our willingness. Are
we willing to sell all, give to the poor, take up our cross of
obedience and follow Jesus? The key word for understanding
the response Jesus wanted from the rich young ruler—and
wants from us—is *willingness*. We never will be free until
we know that if He asked that of us, we would be willing
to accept His terms.

Third, only the Spirit of the Lord can make us willing to
be made willing. When the disciples faced the human impossibility of responding to the challenge of putting the kingdom
first, Jesus said, "With man it is impossible, but not with
God; for with God all things are possible."

No one, rich or poor, educated or uneducated, cultured
or uncultured, young or old, enters the kingdom unless he
or she is called and drawn by the Spirit. The realization of
our need, our conversion, the gift of faith, growth in the
kingdom, and power to live a faithful life—all are gifts given
by sheer grace. That realization brings us to a humble prayer:
"Lord, Your challenge is beyond me. I'm not willing, but I
know You can do the impossible and make me willing. Set
me free from the bind of anything that holds me in bondage

and keeps me from making You Lord of all I am and have!"
That quality of prayer will prepare us for the final step.

Fourth, having put the Lord first, we are ready for the
adventure of seeking His will in the use of all we have for
His glory. That begins with the basics of tithing and giving
to the needs of others. Then we can discover the secret of
being made managers of the inflow and outgo of the financial
resources the Lord entrusts to us. He provides what He wants
to guide us to give. There is no joy more exhilarating than
being surprised constantly by the supply He pours out for
the serendipities of being His agents of compassion to the
economically and spiritually poor all around us and in the
world.

Our Eternal Treasure

With the treasure of eternal life secure in heaven, we can
be the treasure chest out of which the Lord shares His love
with others. We will have made it through the eye of the
needle. And knowing the pain of divided loyalties in the eye
of the needle, we have no need to load up the camel and get
caught again.

Dorothy Sayers, in *The Man Born to Be King*, catches the
dynamic joy of life beyond the eye of the needle. Judas asks
Matthew what happened to all his possessions. Matthew re-
sponds, "I never gave 'em a thought. . . . Then my brother
hunted me up and asked me what I thought I was doing.
'Sell the whole lot up,' I said, 'or do what you like. I'm
done with it.' . . . And I'm having a wonderful time."

To be willing to do that is the secret of staying out of the
eye of the needle.

CHAPTER FIVE

Now it happened as they journeyed on the road, that someone said to Him, "Lord, I will follow You wherever You go." And Jesus said to him, "Foxes have holes and birds of the air have nests, but the Son of Man has nowhere to lay His head." Then He said to another, "Follow Me." But he said, "Lord, let me first go and bury my father." Jesus said to him, "Let the dead bury their own dead, but you go and preach the kingdom of God." And another also said, "Lord, I will follow You, but let me first go and bid them farewell who are at my house." But Jesus said to him, "No one, having put his hand to the plow, and looking back, is fit for the kingdom of God."

(Luke 9:57–62)

PREEMPTED BY PRIORITIES

Jim's voice was a strange combination of wistfulness and challenge as he asked me, "Does Christ have favorites? Why do some Christians radiate such joy while others seem so grim and uptight? Does Christ bless some people more than others?"

I resisted the temptation to answer until I knew what was behind the question. It was obvious that Jim was not putting me on. He really wanted to know. So I asked, "Jim, is that sort of a general question? Or do you have something more specific in mind?"

"Well," he answered thoughtfully, "I guess it's really my own personal question. Some Christians I know are vital and dynamic. But the Christian faith has never been that exciting to me. About six months ago, I heard you tell on television about the joy people in your church are discovering. So I decided to come and see for myself. I've been here every

Sunday since. You're right—there are a lot of joyful Christians here. What's the secret?"

In just those few words, Jim had given me an important clue. He had been in the worship services for six months. That's at least twenty-four Sundays in which an invitation had been given for people to commit their lives to Christ. I could have put him on the defensive by asking why he hadn't responded, so I put my request a different way. "Jim, tell me, when did you become a Christian and what's happened since?"

"That's just it. . . . I can't pinpoint a time when I became a Christian."

Jim went on to share a story I hear often. He had been raised in a church in his hometown, attended a Christian college, married a fine woman from a Christian family, and begun a career as an engineer. Now he has a lovely family, lives in a beautiful home, and appears to be a successful, respected person.

After hearing his story, I said, "My friend, week after week you've heard me talk about the secret of receiving Christ's joy. I've said that fullness of joy is the result of receiving Christ's love and forgiveness and being filled with His Spirit, and all we have to do to begin is accept His gift and give ourselves unreservedly to Him. How have you felt when you've heard me give that invitation?"

"Well, to be honest," Jim said, "I've had a different question each week. What would my wife think? What would Christ require of me if I did commit my life to Him? Would my friends think I'd become a religious fanatic? Would I lose control of my life? By the time I've mulled over the question I pose to myself each week, the service is finished and I can put off the challenge until the next Sunday. But now I've run out of questions—excuses—I guess."

Jim and I went on to talk a long time that day, and he

did surrender his life to Christ. The joy he had longed for is being given him in greater measure than he'd imagined possible. And now he wonders why he had put it off so long. Unfortunately, churches are filled with people like Jim. They become so adept at evading Christ's call to discipleship that they don't hear it anymore.

The Conjunction That Resists

There's a three-letter word, a conjunction of condition, that we use repeatedly to resist a two-word hard saying of Jesus, "Follow me." The word is "but." We want to become His followers, but. . . .

Eventually, though, we "butt up" against our "buts." We all have personal reasons for saying "but." The other Jesus is constantly seeking to preempt our particular set of priorities with His call to follow Him. Our "buts" keep us from following Him. Actually, we try to preempt His priorities.

In Luke 9:57–62 we meet three men who responded to Jesus' "Follow me" with different expressions of reservation. The first two did not use the conjunction; yet it was expressed in their attitudes. The third stated His "but" quite openly. How Jesus dealt with all three shows us how He preempts our priorities. His responses give us three more hard sayings that reveal the deeper meaning of His call to commitment.

The Cost of Following the Master

The Master was on His way to Jerusalem and the cross. Now His oft-repeated "Follow me" was quickened in intensity and urgency. It also carried much more demanding implications of the cost of discipleship. With Him were the inner circle of the disciples who had heard and responded to the call. Walking alongside were others who were still uncertain about their response. Luke tells us that as they were on their way through Samaria enroute to Jerusalem, one Samaritan village refused to receive Jesus.

We join the group as they move on down the road, and we watch the reactions of the would-be followers. The first pushes his way through the group and pulls Jesus by the arm. Jesus stops and looks at him intently. The whole procession pauses to listen to their conversation.

"Lord, I will follow You wherever You go," the man says proudly. We notice from his attire that he is a scribe.[1] That's quite a promise of faithfulness from one of the scribes who, along with the Pharisees, had so constantly disputed Jesus' claims and so forcefully discredited His ministry. It must have taken a great deal of courage for him to leave the ranks of Jesus' critics and join His group of followers. Perhaps he had come along to get more evidence against Him. Whatever the case, he's obviously had a change of attitude.

Jesus' response is startling. "Foxes have holes and birds of the air have nests, but the Son of Man has nowhere to lay His head." Isn't that a bit abrupt for this scribe's first expression of loyalty? But Jesus sees something we haven't observed. We're so satisfied with whatever little loyalty we've given Him and so delighted with the least response of people today that we want to compliment the scribe for the first stirring in him of desire to be a follower. Not Jesus. He wanted the scribe to count the cost.

And he wanted something else. The scribes and Pharisees had rejected Jesus' claim that He was the Messiah—the Son of Man—sent by God to reveal perfect manhood and with divine authority to judge and forgive sins. His deliberate use

---

1. "A certain scribe," Matt. 8:19.

of the title "Son of Man" in His response to the scribe indicates that Jesus sensed what was lacking. Apparently, the scribe admired Jesus as an inspiring leader, but he hadn't accepted His teaching. He was not committed to Jesus as the divine Son of Man. His "but" of reservation, though not spoken, was expressed by what he didn't say.

Further, we sense that what troubled Jesus about the man was his self-assertiveness. While He hadn't specifically said to the man, "Follow Me," the scribe assumed he was worthy of that invitation.

Jesus often confronted this kind of human presumption. This man obviously had his own set of personal priorities. Probably he was still preoccupied with his religious legalism and traditionalism. He had not come to grips with what Jesus had clearly said about being "delivered into the hands of men" (Luke 9:44), the inevitability of the cross, and the childlike humility he wanted as the measure of greatness in His followers (Luke 9:48).

This scribe is like so many Christians today whose religious enthusiasm or participation in the church has become their best defense against making an unreserved commitment of their total lives to Christ.

A Life-Changing Personal Experience

I know. My own early years as a Christian were filled with self-generated religious enthusiasm rather than self-surrendering, honest commitment. I was carried along by the excitement of being part of a movement with adventuresome friends. When I went to New College in Edinburgh, Scotland, to complete my postgraduate studies, my relationship to Christ was bordered north, south, east, and west by Lloyd. My inner need to have Christ transform my personality had been avoided in the frantic rush of Christian activities, meetings, and the thrill of being a clergyperson. With all of this busyness, I hadn't really faced my deep need for the transforming power of Christ's cross, nor had I taken up my own cross of absolute obedience.

One day in a class taught by Thomas Torrence, I evaded the penetrating thrust of his teaching with carefully stated questions. Dr. Torrence saw my need. "Mr. Ogilvie, you can't sneak around Golgotha. You must die!"

I listened in shocked attention while my professor explained what it meant to die to self—pride, plans, priorities, personality. It meant giving over my total life to Christ, including my insecurity, which came across in self-assertiveness. With the surrender of my life, Christ's death for me on Calvary would not only become real, but my only hope.

After the class, Dr. Torrence helped me to make the surrender he'd described so vividly. That was the beginning of authentic joy for me. What happened that winter day in 1955 was only the beginning of the ever-increasing joy I've experienced through the years.

It also accounts for why, throughout my ministry, I've shared, taught, and preached the absolute necessity of death to self as an irreducible requisite in any authentic commitment to Christ. We must die with Him in our own Calvary before we can be raised with Him in a resurrection to new life and an infilling of His Spirit.

I see the transforming power of that experience as the great need in contemporary Christianity in America. The lack of that death to self and subsequent infilling of the Spirit explains the powerlessness of so many church people. It also accounts for the absence of joyous discipleship. Churches are overpopulated with people like the scribe whose self-motivated religion was keeping him from true commitment. The obstacle is an unspoken, but firmly held, defensive "but."

Secondary Loyalties

Let's rejoin Jesus on the road to Jerusalem as He turns to another man and gives the clarion call, "Follow Me." We wonder at the man's glib response, "Lord, let me first go and bury my father." Since the man has been traveling with Jesus for several days and since people were usually buried before sunset of the day of their death, it seems improbable that the man's father had died that morning. Had the man joined Jesus' band with the intention of leaving momentarily to go home for the burial? That's unlikely.

Rather, the man was using a proverbial saying about the tradition of caring for an aged person until death. The saying is still used today in the Middle East. What the man meant was, "I want to follow You, Master, *but* I have an aged father. I must take care of him until he dies. Then I will follow You as Your disciple." While his father was alive, he would not leave him to follow Jesus.

Now we can understand why Jesus answered the man the way He did: "Let the dead bury their own dead, but you go and preach the kingdom of God." The obvious meaning of the proverb "Let the dead bury the dead" is that the spiritually dead should bury the physically dead. Jesus has met the man on his level: a proverb for a proverbial saying. He sees the man's easy dexterity with glib excuses. If he is that concerned with care for his father, why is he not at home now?

What does this exchange mean to us? For one thing, it certainly exposes our quickly worded excuses, whatever they are. On a deeper level, however, I can't help but ask if Jesus would call us to neglect our family responsibilities. Most of us have obligations to family and friends. Are we to walk away from these duties to serve Christ?

The Real Issue

It's what we put first that is the real issue. The other Jesus confronts us with the absolute necessity of making our commitment to Him and then sharing His love with others as our first priority. Then we can seek His will for our responsibilities to the people of our lives. Whenever anyone becomes more important to us than Jesus, we have made that person a little god. And when his or her plans for us, opinions of us, or reservations about how we live our faith dominate our thinking, we lose our freedom to follow Christ.

So often, people in our lives try to control us by affirming or criticizing our behavior. And because our feelings of insecurity create in us such a desperate need for their approval, we are tempted to let their opinions determine the shape of our commitment to Christ.

When that is allowed to happen, both we and the people around us suffer. We use them as excuses for not following Christ and His priorities unreservedly. Then we have very little to give them. But when we put Him first, He fills us with His love and power. Then we are equipped to care more profoundly and to serve more unselfishly than when we put people before Christ.

A woman who had fought her husband's commitment to Christ later said, "I lost a husband I could control and manipulate and gained a free man who loves and cares for me in a way beyond my fondest dreams. When I saw what Christ did with my husband when he put Him first, I wanted to find the same joy. Finally that led me to Christ. I shudder to think what might have happened if my husband had given in to my badgering. Think what I would have missed!"

That challenges us to think of people whom we have allowed to hold us back. And what about people we may be keeping from pulling out all the stops as followers of Christ?

I remember a "Christian" marketing analyst who told me I'd never make it as a television communicator unless I changed my thrust from Christ-centered, biblical messages to more acceptable "pop" psychology. My answer was, "If changing what I've done for thirty years is the price of easy success, then I'm prepared not to make it. But I'm counting on the fact that people in America long for Christ's love and power. I'd rather *raise* the spiritually dead than *bury* the spiritually dead!"

Christ had to come first above expansion or ratings or audience response as they are calculated in the media world. And only He is the source of the program's growth from one station in Los Angeles a few years ago to a nationally syndicated ministry with hundreds of thousands of viewers each week.

The Trouble with Looking Backward

Let's look in again on the band of disciples and inquirers who were walking along the road with Jesus. After a time He turned to another potential disciple and said, "Follow Me." This man's excuse tumbled out almost as quickly as the previous man's equivocation. Note, however, that his "but" is not implied; it is flatly stated. "Lord, I will follow You, *but* let me first go and bid them farewell who are at my house."

Upon first hearing, that sounds like the excuse of the second man. He has to take care of an aging father; this one has to say goodbye to his family and friends at home. We discover the difference in their excuses from Jesus' discerning response. To this third man He says, "No one, having put his hand to the plow, and looking back, is fit for the kingdom of God." In answering as He did, Jesus gives us another one of His hard sayings.

In our mind's eye we can see what would happen if a person looked back while plowing a furrow. The furrow would be crooked. Plowing a straight furrow requires keeping the eyes focused on a point out ahead. Jesus' words "looking back" really mean "constantly looking back" in the Greek. Anyone who plowed that way through a field would surely run a zigzag course.

By use of this simple agricultural proverb, Jesus has given this man and us a very profound spiritual truth. Constantly looking back makes us unfit for the demanding challenges of not only the future, but the present. The word for "fit" in Greek is *euthetos*, meaning "ready for use, adapted, well-placed." The man who wants to go home to say farewell to his family, friends, and neighbors isn't really ready to follow Jesus as the leader of his life. He is more concerned about what he has to leave behind.

The Master sees beneath the words of the man's "but." He understands with divine insight what's in the man's heart. If he goes home, he will probably never come back. Jesus senses that he wants to go home to do more than say farewell. The word "farewell" in Greek is *apotaxasthai* from *apotassō*. It means "to detach" or "to separate," but it also can be used as a military term for assignments to a detachment of soldiers.

I suspect the man wants to straighten out his relationships so he can be sure everything will go according to his plans. Perhaps he has some broken relationships to mend and perhaps some hurts to heal. Here is a man who has his anchor stuck in the mud of the unforgiven and the unresolved. He is thinking about the past rather than the future.

So often we set limits on our own response to the other Jesus because of what's happened to us in the past. We constantly try to "fix it" with either guilt or self-justification. Again and again, we go back over unhealed memories or make a determined effort to repeat past successes. We constantly try to atone for the first and draw false security from the second. We make the past a haunting monster or a false idol. In either case, we are still in control and constantly looking back. What we miss is the sublime opportunity of the present and the exciting adventure of the future.

Like this third man, a lot of us find it difficult to accept Christ's forgiveness for past failures. We think there's something more we can do to set things right. It is no less debilitating to hang onto our glories of the past, thinking that we have to achieve continued success to qualify for the kingdom. And equally frustrating is our inability to entrust to Christ the future welfare of loved ones. We entertain the idea that they won't make it unless we remain in charge of their destiny.

When we're looking for excuses to resist a commitment to Christ, there are so many worthy things that we can say we must do before we surrender our lives. And after we have committed our lives, it's equally tempting to think that Christ has stopped loving us because of something we've done and that He will return His acceptance only after we complete some act that we've set up as a qualification.

The Joy of Surrendering Our Excuses

We all have our own personal, carefully rehearsed brand of "buts" in response to Christ's hard saying "Follow Me." We don't know what happened to those three men on the road after they offered their excuses, and that doesn't matter. What's important is how we respond. After the three men in our story have turned away, the Master looks at us. Suddenly we know that no excuse will work. We long for the joy and peace that only unreserved response to Him makes possible. And with all our hearts we cry out,

> The dearest idol I have known,
>   Whate'er that idol be;
> Help me to tear it from Thy throne,
> And worship only thee.[1]

The Greatest Miracle

I opened this chapter with the story of Jim's excuses and final breakthrough to the joy of commitment. Mary's story, though different, also shows what can happen when Christ overcomes our excuses.

"It's got to be a miracle!" Mary said to me after a Sunday morning service a few weeks ago. "I've been on a quest for an authentic spiritual life for years. A hunger's been gnawing at me, an anxious longing to know the Lord. But I've been afraid of what it might cost me. I've tried so many churches and so many self-help, human potential groups. Nothing seemed to work. Christ's words 'Follow me' still haunted me.

"A few weeks ago one of your members invited me to come here to church with her. For five weeks I've listened to your invitation to commit my life to Christ. And today I couldn't remain in my pew any longer. I got up, went forward, and accepted Christ's call. Now He is my Savior and Lord. And He's got all of me that there is."

---

1. William Cowper, "O for a Closer Walk with God," 1772.

Many people think of miracles as some physical healing or impossible intervention in some problem. For Mary, after all the years of searching and making excuses, the greatest miracle was that she could respond. She had thought it was something she had to do. Actually, the Lord set her free to surrender her life. And with all the resistance of the years, it's amazing that He got through to her so she could hear that she is loved, forgiven, and cherished. And now that she's responded she says, "I feel great all over. It's a real miracle!"

CHAPTER SIX

Is it not written in your law, "I said, 'You are gods' "? If He called them gods, to whom the word of God came (and the Scripture cannot be broken), do you say of Him whom the Father sanctified and sent into the world, "You are blaspheming," because I said, "I am the Son of God"?

(John 10:34–36)

THE FEAR OF WINNING

The fear of winning? Who's afraid of winning? Doesn't everyone want to be a winner?

Definitely not—surprising as it may seem, our actions indicate that many of us are gripped by an inner panic about winning. Even though we glibly affirm, "Everybody loves a winner!" few of us think of ourselves, much less cheer ourselves on, as winners. As a matter of fact, some of us unconsciously do the things that will keep us from winning. We sabotage ourselves.

This is not to say that we necessarily set up a planned strategy for losing. But inadvertently we may do and say things that keep us from winning in the challenges, relationships and responsibilities of life. One way or another we give up before a goal is accomplished or a task or project is finished. The truth is that many of us are more committed to losing than to winning.

We hear a lot about the fear of failure these days. I've even heard people admit they didn't attempt something because they were afraid of failing. But I'm convinced that's only the flip side of the fear of winning.

As I've thought about it, it would seem that many of us are conditioned by low self-esteem to feel that we don't deserve to win. I've known people who were so crippled by the negative attitudes of parents, siblings, friends, and significant teachers and leaders in their formative years they never expect to win. There are also those who fear the responsibility of winning. But, whatever the reason, most all of us just don't think we're worthy of winning. We choreograph our own failures by performing at less than our best.

Why is this? In this chapter I want us to wrestle with why we are afraid of winning. Then I'd like to consider one of Jesus' hard sayings that shows us our full potential as winners. To prepare the way for that we need to consider what it really means to win.

False and True Ideas of Winning

First, let me tell you what I don't mean by winning. I'm not referring to the obvious trophies of success. It's not winning all of life's arguments. Winning is not controlling and manipulating people to get what we want. It isn't being "top dog" or always rising to positions of power. And it's not financial success and security, or simply receiving the cheering accolades and approval of people.

The kind of winning I'm talking about is much more profound. It is an inner quality that transforms our outer attitudes toward life. For Christians, winning is fulfilling the purpose for which we were born. It is being the person the Lord intends for us to be. Winning is living at peak performance, to the maximum level of our individual capability. We never realize our full potential until we experience this sublime joy of knowing that we are loved and cherished by the Lord and receive the fullness and freedom of His Spirit.

True winning, then, is desiring, discovering, and doing the Lord's ultimate will and following His daily guidance. Winning is living in the liberating assurance that we are sons and daughters of God and have been chosen to fulfill a unique destiny.

The wonderful good news for us, though, is that, as Christians, we are running a race that we've already won. We don't compete to win the Lord's acceptance or affirmation. That's already been given in full measure. Instead, we are called to run with Him as winners who have been given the crown of victory.

This is the confidence we are to have as we face life's opportunities. In our personal relationships, in our work, and in the accomplishment of the particular assignments the Lord gives us, we are meant to live with full faith that, in His own way and timing, His plans and purposes will be accomplished through us. He wants to enable us to win in our calling to love others profoundly and succeed in the work He gives us to do.

Sounds great, doesn't it? Then why do so few Christians think of themselves as winners? I believe it is because so much of our psychological conditioning has prepared us to expect to lose or, at least, to live a frustrating life of ups and downs.

The Other Jesus Confronts the Fear of Winning

The other Jesus—the Jesus of confrontation, the Jesus of hard sayings—wants to heal us of this self-depreciating, self-destructive feeling of not being worthy of winning. He wants to break the hold of whatever it is in our past that makes us fear getting on with being spiritually successful children of God.

We see this vividly illustrated in one of the most dramatic and tension-filled scenes in the Gospel of John as Jesus gave His listeners and us a hard saying that speaks directly to the fear of winning.

Our own experiences of resisting Jesus in His efforts to accomplish His positive purpose in us help us to understand the fierce opposition to Him during His ministry. His own people, the Jews, were challenged by His call to them to rediscover their true destiny. John reports in chapter 10 of his Gospel that Jesus startled the people with both His declaration of His purpose and the source of His power. He clearly told them that He had come from the Father so that they might have life and have it abundantly. That promise was linked to His claim that He was the Son of God. "The Father and I are one," He said boldly.

A Charge of Blasphemy and Jesus' Response

That so enraged the Jews one day during the Feast of Dedication in Jerusalem that they became a self-appointed lynch mob. Charging Him with blasphemy, they took stones in hand to put Him to death. In the ensuing verbal exchange, Jesus set forth one of His hardest sayings. When understood, it becomes a powerful antidote to the fear of winning.

The hard saying was Jesus' response to the charge that He had blasphemed by claiming to be equal with God. He said, "Is it not written in your law, 'I said, "You are gods" '? If He called them gods, to whom the word of God came (and the Scripture cannot be broken), do you say of Him whom the Father sanctified and sent into the world, 'You are blaspheming' because I said, 'I am the Son of God'?" (John 10:34–36).

Jesus' knowledge of the Scriptures shines through magnificently. In this hard saying, He quoted from Psalm 82. The psalm had been directed to Israel's judges who, centuries before, had misused their calling to interpret God's righteousness and justice among the people. In the psalm they are called by the Hebrew word *elohim*, meaning "judges" or "gods."

But Jesus, employing the context of the whole psalm, went for the jugular vein of an even deeper issue. Quoting verse 6 in direct response to the Jews' charge of blasphemy, He used it to confront them with an even greater blasphemy: the depreciation of their calling to be gods, judges, and sons and daughters of the Lord God. "I said, 'You are gods, and all of you are children of the Most High' " (Ps. 82:6).

After quoting that verse of God's affirmation of His people, Jesus went on to pose a very poignant question. In essence He asked, "If God called the ancient leaders *elohim*, gods, and all of the people sons of God, why do you say I am blaspheming by having said I am the Son of God? Scripture is sacred authority, and Scripture calls all God's people 'sons.' On a purely human level, therefore, My claim is not presumptuous."

Jesus did not leave the matter there. He pressed on boldly, with specific evidence. He pointed out that His works, His divinely empowered signs, and miracles should be the final basis of the authority of His claim that He was not only a son, but *the* Son who had been sanctified and sent into the world by the Father. "If I do not do the works of My Father, do not believe Me; but if I do, though you do not believe Me, believe the works, that you may know and believe that the Father is in Me, and I in Him" (John 10:37–38).

Many who accused the Master that day had seen His signs and wonders, and the rest had certainly heard about them. They all had been given the opportunity to believe in Him because of His works. Even then, they had resisted, brushing aside their knowledge of His works and ridiculing the convincing claim of His words that He was one with the Father. Why?

Depreciated Glory

My guess is that, underneath the surface, Jesus' accusers were distressed not only by His claims for Himself, but also by what He claimed for them as sons and daughters of God. So often we analyze the resistance as pride and self-sufficiency. But what else is their behavior other than the outward manifestation of profound inner insecurity? The Jews were suffering from what I call depreciated glory. They were afraid of winning as God's loved and cherished people.

I suspect that Jesus quoted that sixth verse of the 82nd Psalm not only to validate His own Sonship, but to remind the Jews of their own. They had depreciated the true glory of that. Instead of experiencing the security of "chosenness" in their ongoing daily living, they rested on what God had done for them in the past as His chosen people. Away from an intimate communion with the Father, they had found their security in rules and regulations and in formalized, ritualistic religion. Their arrogant legalism was focused in judgmentalism. Jesus had exposed this condition in calling them to the abundant life now and eternal life forever. Because they were really "down" on themselves and discouraged about their national plight as a people, they were not "up" to receive the inspiration of what Jesus told them about Himself and about their own potential. As He said later on in His ministry, they did not grasp the fact that His coming was "the time of their visitation" (Luke 19:44).

The Jews who sought to stone Jesus possessed none of the awe and wonder expressed by the psalmist in Psalm 8. The affirming term *elohim*, "gods, judges," is used in this psalm in a way that should have given the Jews an unshakable sense of self-esteem about who they were in God's plan. Reflect on the psalmist's adoration of the glory of God and the greatness He had allocated to His chosen people: "When I consider Your heavens, the work of Your fingers, / The moon and the stars, which You have ordained, / What is man that You are mindful of him / And the son of man that You visit him? / For You have made him a little lower than the angels, / And You have crowned him with glory and honor" (Ps. 8:3–5).

The word for "angels" is also *elohim* in the Hebrew text. It can mean the judges referred to in Psalm 82:1, suggesting that the quality of spiritual sensitivity and discernment intended by God for the judges of Israel is offered to all of God's people. Or, it can be interpreted that He has created His people with a status a little lower than the heavenly hosts who share the vision and praise of His eternal glory. Or, more pointedly, the verse can be translated, "Yet Thou hast made him little less than God and hast crowned Him with glory and honor." That's the way it's rendered in both the New American Standard Bible and the Revised Standard Version.

God's Amazing Confidence in Us

At whatever level we choose to translate the word *elohim*, we are stunned by the amazing confidence God has placed in us. He came in Jesus Christ to help us recover the courage-building confidence of that high status. He is not against us; He is for us. As people created a little lower than Himself, He wants us to know Him and enjoy Him. In Jesus, we see what that means. He lived among us as God's Son so that we might know the delight of being sons and daughters. If we really accepted that, it would offset the debilitating experiences of our past which have contributed to our fear of winning.

Because the Jews who hassled Jesus that day had lost the security of that truth, they were unconsciously driven to assume their own failure. They were part of the depression that gripped Israel in national paranoia. Living under the suppression of Rome, they looked for a Messiah who would wield military might and reestablish their political grandeur of the past. They had a distorted idea of winning. Instead of seeing it as participation in a spiritual kingdom of God's grace, righteousness, and justice, they thought in terms of a political kingdom and power.

Following the destruction of Jerusalem in 586 B.C., through the long years of the Exile and their subsequent subjugation under one conquerer after another, the Jews had struggled continually with their identity as the chosen people of God. Jesus came with a very different revelation of the kingdom of God. Bristling in defensiveness, they expressed their paranoia in refusing to accept it or Him. In essence, they were really committed to failure instead of victory. They were so discouraged in their long waiting for the Messiah that they could not recognize Him when He came. They had misread the prophecies of His coming and sought a kingdom radically different from the one predicted in their Scriptures.

As we do when we are afraid of winning and so are committed to our failures, the Jews devalued their true destiny and robbed themselves of the wonder and willingness of humility rooted in God-centered esteem. That quality is absolutely necessary if we are to grasp the opportunities of life with confidence and joy.

Now we are ready to draw the implications for us of Jesus' hard saying and our own brand of the fear of winning. The other Jesus will not allow us to perpetuate the negative self-image of the past but comes to us to make us new people. He frees us of the foreboding experiences which have contributed to our commitment to losing in life's privileges and perplexities. When we surrender our past to Him, He heals the memories of what makes us down on ourselves. He helps us to forgive the people who have constricted our idea of what we can do and become. He lifts us out of the mire of self-criticism that feeds on the negative messages received from others in our formative years as well as in the present. And, as we said in chapter 1, He abides within us as the Lord of the master control center of our minds. He gives us a new picture of ourselves as loved and a new image of ourselves as winners who can love others and who can succeed in what He guides us to dare to do.

I know that, from my own life and observation of people through the years. Perhaps the reason I feel so much empathy for people with a fear of winning is because of my own experience with the problem.

My Own Story

For me, the fear of winning had its roots in an incident in my teenage years, when an experience that should have been one of my most positive turned out to be one of the most frightening. Through the inspiring influence and excellent coaching of a speech teacher, John Davies, I was able to feel the first delicious taste of healthy self-esteem as I won a national oratorical contest.

Upon my return to my hometown of Kenosha, Wisconsin, I was given a parade. Then, after an assembly in my high school to recognize my first-place trophy, I started home. As I walked along, thinking about all that had happened, I was excited. With the scholarship I'd won, I knew for the first time that I'd be able to go on to college. There was a new confidence in my step, and I whistled happily as I thought about the new future now open to me.

Before long I reached an alley I often took as a shortcut on my way to and from school. In the alley, darkened by the shadows of late afternoon, I met a group of my buddies. They weren't at all pleased with my success. In fact, they were very angry. Ridiculing my victory, they accused me of being arrogant, a sissy giving speeches and no longer a part of the old pack. Then they proceeded to rough me up, stinging me with hard-hitting punches and abusive language.

Finally I was able to pull away and run out of the alley toward home. In time, of course, my physical bruises healed, but I decided never to be in a position of using whatever talents I might have if it made others feel insecure. To insure that I would not be hurt that way again, I put a cap on my potential.

That event was soon buried in my subconscious. In college I became a Christian and made a decision to become a pastor. Seminary and postgraduate school years passed quickly, and soon I was the pastor of a church. It was then that I became aware of an inner fear of winning. Inner self-doubt contradicted any outward signs of success. I could not enjoy doing well and would usually downgrade my accomplishments, which made me all the more self-conscious.

During that time, I worked hard to escape what I falsely identified as a fear of failure. But in reality, it was winning I feared, as I unconsciously reacted to the old alley gang.

The tightly clamped cap on myself was still in place. At the same time, I overpolished the outward gifts of speech, which sometimes made me come across as superficial. The thing I wanted least—criticism for being too slick—I actually brought on myself.

The Secrets of Healing and Praise

I'm very thankful the Lord didn't allow that pattern to go on for very long. During the first year of my ministry He led me to discover two vital secrets of spiritual growth: the healing of memories and the liberating power of praise. I had begun my studies in both while a postgraduate student, and now what I had learned became a personal experience.

I began praying about my fear of failing and asked the Lord to help me see what was causing it. One morning during my quiet time, the frightening memory of the alley came back in full force. Rather than pushing it away I allowed it to come back into full focus. What had happened eleven years before seemed like yesterday. I whispered a prayer: "Lord, please heal this memory." A thought formed in my mind with compelling force. It could not have been more gripping if I had heard the Lord speak audibly. I was afraid of success, not failure! The limits I had placed on myself were keeping me from enjoying winning. I got on my knees and asked the Lord to release me from that bondage. I will never forget the peace and joy I felt.

At this same time in my spiritual pilgrimage I was also discovering the releasing power of praise in all circumstances. I found that the secret of getting free of worry over problems and difficulties was to praise the Lord for them and for whatever He wanted to teach me through them. I also discovered that giving Him praise is the antidote to false pride, and that my previous unwillingness to enjoy the talents and gifts

He had entrusted to me was lack of praise. Praising the Lord for His blessings to me released me from either self-negation or self-aggrandizement. Over a period of spiritual experimentation with praise for all things, I began to enjoy being me and giving Him all the glory for any success. The cap I had put on my potential was pried loose and eventually blown off; the fear of winning was healed.

My own painful struggle with the fear of winning and my eventual victory over it have enabled me to discern this problem in others. Several of these people come to mind now as I write.

Jaundiced John

A friend in the Midwest whom I've come to call "Jaundiced John" simply does not know how to enjoy the Lord's blessing in both good and difficult times. John attended a retreat I led in the Chicago area recently. When I learned he was coming, I have to admit to bracing myself for a fresh outpouring of woe.

"How are you, John?" I asked.

"Great!" he replied, to my surprise. But then he went on, "It won't last. I've learned that when things go well, it won't be very long before I get hit with trouble again. That's the way it always works—up times are followed by tough times."

Now, John isn't a manic depressive who suffers from mood swings. Actually, he's a fairly well-adjusted Christian. But he has a serious flaw in his thinking. He just can't handle winning for long. And here's the startling thing: over the years, I've noticed that John unconsciously does things to insure that his good times won't last.

If things are going well with his wife and family, it isn't long before he says or does something that creates havoc in the home. On the job, he has always managed to keep things stirred up. Unfortunately, it never occurs to John that he invites trouble and criticism. Instead, he has always blamed everybody else for what happened to him.

The few days of the retreat provided the opportunity for some long conversations with John. I felt that our years of friendship gave me the right to talk out with him his yo-yo existence of ups and downs. Finally, after several long walks during which we dug into the problem, we were able to trace the pattern back to John's dad.

"John," his dad used to say to him when he was growing up, "don't get cocky when you succeed. The Lord will knock the props from under you. You can always be certain that hard times will follow good times as sure as night follows the day."

Even though John believed in Christ, his unrecognized need to fulfill his dad's negative programming was dominating his life. When he finally understood that and expressed a desire to do something about it, we were able to pray together. John began to see that he was controlled more by his dad's distorted idea of punishment than by the Lord's power to help him triumph in life's delights *and* difficulties, both of which could be a source of blessing. John didn't have to cause the difficulties to fulfill his dad's prophecy about life. By the end of the retreat, my friend had made a start in being a winner.

Several other people I know are just discovering the causes of their fear of winning. As you will see, those causes can be varied but all are debilitating and frustrating.

The Influence of the Inner Child of the Past

Take Glen, for example. He constantly scuttled his own chances of winning because of his father's lack of success.

Each time Glen was about to crest in his career, he would do something that denied him the promotion and recognition he had earned. Buried deep below the surface of his mind was the feeling that he had no right to overtake his father, and he felt tremendous guilt each time he had an opportunity to succeed.

Tim, unlike Glen, had a father who was both successful and famous. But the one thing Tim's dad never had time to give him was a sense of his own worth. Tim grew up in the heady atmosphere of pressure to achieve, yet he was never able to please his dad. Today, as a grown man and a relatively successful businessman, Tim still feels a sense of inadequacy and frequently does things to prove that he is inadequate. Those around him pick up on his negative feelings about himself and support his opinion.

Judy is the daughter of an outstanding lawyer. Her father didn't hide his disappointment that Judy, his only child, hadn't been born a boy who could step into his shoes. She tried hard, though, and was a straight "A" student in college and law school. After graduation, she became a lawyer in a firm away from her hometown. Though her career has gone very well, she is not sure she will ever really be a success. The one thing she can't be is a man. Judy's dad says he's proud of her, but he has never suggested that she should come to work for him or prepare to take over his firm.

Judy's mother believed a woman's place was in the home cheering and supporting her husband while keeping busy in church and community activities. She had not been in favor of Judy's desire to go to law school or have a career. She let her know that she wished she'd settle down, get married, and have a family.

So Judy was torn. She wanted to succeed to convince her dad a woman could make it in the practice of law; at the same time success would not please her mother. All that turmoil was hidden beneath the surface of Judy's very sophisticated, professional manner. She wanted to win and yet feared it. Only recently has she begun to think about what it means to be a winner in terms of the Lord's purpose for her life. It was a tremendous release for her when she committed her life to Him and decided that He was the only person she had to please.

Alice's problem with winning was focused in her relationship with her husband. Her image of what it meant to be a wife was tied to the bossy way her mother related to her father. Alice and I talked over the pushy things she had said and done that had enraged her husband. It was a shock to Alice to discover she was actually committed to failing in her marriage. When she finally faced up to her fear of winning, she was able to see that she'd been hanging onto the familiar, but self-destructive habit of mothering her husband. When she began focusing on a new image of herself winning in Jesus' style, the old pattern was broken.

Negative Criticism

A host of people I've known through the years, and others I'm associated with today, have such an ingrained negative view of themselves that they can't believe they deserve to win at life. Their surface experience of Christ has not healed this attitude, nor has activity in the church. Their spiritual life simply becomes an extension of this self-depreciation. They can't grasp the amazing grace and abundant life Jesus offers. Instead, they keep doing things that reaffirm their intent to keep Him at arm's length.

Many of these people have suffered from negative criticism. There's enough of that to go around in most every family, circle of friends and even the church. And when we let the criticism of the significant people in our lives fester inside us, we eventually become the worst that others communicate to us about ourselves. In time, we have a fully developed case of the fear of winning.

The amazing thing about all these people I've described is that they are Christians. The other Jesus disturbs this depreciation of the glory entrusted to us. He unsettles us not only with what we've done with the gift of life, but also with the smallness of the limits we put on what we believe we can become. He does not rub our souls raw with reminders of our past sins; He inspires us with a vision of our untapped potential of greatness for the future.

Paul—The Loser Who Became a Winner

The Apostle Paul is a challenging example of what Jesus can do to transform a loser into a winner. The Saul of Tarsus we meet prior to his conversion is a classic example of a religious person who is still the author, director, stage manager, and central actor in the drama of his own self-defeat. Saul was compulsively committed in his resistance to Jesus.

But when Saul met the risen, reigning Jesus on the road to Damascus, a process of transformation began and continued through the preparation for his life ministry of spreading the Gospel. Jesus took up residence in his mind. The old man, Saul, whose angry judgmentalism had brought him to the brink of despair, was exorcised, and the new man in Christ, Paul, was formed in him.

In Romans 7 the apostle explains the collusive influence of evil and our sinful nature in producing the paralysis of the fear of winning. "For the good I will to do, I do not do; but the evil I will not do, that I practice" (Rom. 7:19). What a vivid description of our plight! Some have argued that Paul was describing his experience prior to conversion; others say that he was identifying the continuing struggle within himself even after commitment to Christ. Many of us would agree with those who suggest that this is a persistent battle with our human nature even after we become Christians.

But it's not a hopeless battle. We can claim with Paul the only hope, "I thank God—through Jesus Christ our Lord. . . . There is therefore now no condemnation to those who are in Christ Jesus who do not walk according to the flesh, but according to the Spirit" (Rom 7:25; 8:1). We don't have to be continually defeated by the failures of the past or by what others have done to shape our self-image as losers. "Walking according to the Spirit" means being filled by and under the control of the living, indwelling Christ. When we courageously dare to examine our self-defeating memories and present patterns, we can be healed and liberated.

That promise is triumphantly stated in 2 Corinthians 5:17: "Therefore, if anyone is in Christ, he is a new creation; old things have passed away; behold, all things have become new." We have been reconciled to God by Christ through the cross. And the living Christ within us continues to show us anything that is crippling us as new creatures in Him. He lifts it from the unconscious to the conscious level so that we can give it to Him and both know and feel we no longer need to insure our own defeat.

And here's some comfort for those of us who are still in the process of realizing a freedom from the fear of winning. At the end of his life, Paul was still seeking greater intimacy with Christ. Though he was imprisoned in Rome, he was a free man in Christ. He wrote what I call his definition of winning. "For to me, to live is Christ . . ." (Phil. 1:21), and, ". . . I also count all things loss for the excellence of the knowledge of Christ . . . that I may know Him and the power of His resurrection . . ." (Phil. 3:8, 10).

Paul could endure hardship and suffering as a part of serving Christ, but he felt no need to bring suffering on himself as an unconscious effort to punish himself for the past. And even to the end, he was willing to confess his desire to press on in Christianity's own special, sublime quality of winning. "Not that I have already attained, or am already perfected; but I press on, that I may lay hold of that for which Christ Jesus has also laid hold of me. . . . One thing I do, forgetting those things which are behind and reaching forward to those things which are ahead, I press toward the goal for the prize of the upward call of God in Christ Jesus" (Phil. 3:12–14).

Christ Can Make Us Winners!

Later, in his second imprisonment just before his execution, the apostle, reflecting on his life in Christ, gave us a motto for winning, "I have fought the good fight, I have finished the race, I have kept the faith" (2 Tim. 4:7).

These words of Paul, inspired by the other Jesus, are the words of a winner. They spur us on in our present lap in the race of life. There's no need to put ourselves down as losers. Living life in Christ is winning in itself. We can say with Paul, "I can do all things through Christ who strengthens me" (Phil. 4:13).

For a Christian, there's no such thing as a "no-win" situation or relationship. We are called to be faithful to our Lord. Even when that means difficulty, we win in seeking to do what He guides and in expressing the joy, love, and hope He provides. The results are up to Him. And instead of piling up one more self-incriminating failure to mock us when the next big challenge comes along, we will press on knowing that in the end we will experience an ultimate victory which will be the climax of a lifetime of winning.

The other Jesus invades the inner being of each of us. His healing touch reaches the child of the past in us with acceptance and affirmation. He tenderly exorcises the crippling memories or negative criticism that make us feel inadequate. He communicates His vision for what we can be, living at the full potential of His power in us. We feel the surge of courage. No longer do we need to will our own failure. We are sons and daughters of God, crowned with glory and honor and free to live without the fear of winning.

CHAPTER SEVEN

I came to send fire on the earth, and how I wish it were already kindled! But I have a baptism to be baptized with, and how distressed I am till it is accomplished!
(Luke 12:49–50)

FIRE DOORS OF THE MIND

One night a few years ago, I was awakened by the ringing of the telephone by my bed. I groped about in the dark for the receiver. Half awake, I mumbled a sleepy "hello."

"The church is on fire!" an excited voice shouted. "I'll be right down," I said, stabbed fully awake by the alarming news.

When I arrived at the church building, the fire department had the blaze under control. After several hours, I returned home and went back to bed.

By then it was dawn and I found it difficult to go back to sleep. When I finally drifted off into half-awake slumber, I was startled into consciousness again with the memory of the words "The church is on fire!" ringing in my ears.

I tossed and turned. Then I began to reflect on the fact that the person who called me hadn't said, "The church building is on fire!" but "The church is on fire!" I thought about how we simultaneously speak of the church as both a building and the fellowship of the followers of Jesus. Church steeples and the Lord's people go together in our minds. But I came to the joyous conclusion that the First Presbyterian Church of Hollywood would have gone right on being the church even if the building we've grown to cherish with fond memories had been burned to the ground.

I smiled to myself as I thought further about how the word "fire" is associated with the Spirit. Spiritual fire is one of the attributes of the Spirit. That led me to think about how much I longed for the church—not only my own, but all churches—to catch fire with the flaming love, joy, enthusiasm, and power of the Spirit. There are no words I want more to hear from people in my congregation, or from friends around the world than "Our church is on fire!" I wondered why we hear that exclamation so seldom from contemporary Christians.

A Modern-Day Parable

With those thoughts on my mind, I was ready to receive the full impact of a contemporary parable later in the morning when I went back to the church building. The fire marshal told me that, for the future safety of the building, he would have to insist that fire doors be installed throughout the structure. "When fire breaks out in an area," he said, "the doors will close automatically so that it will not spread throughout the entire building."

Now that the fire-door system has been installed, we have doors in all the corridors and stairways which will close instantly if ever there is the least evidence of fire in any part of the building.

You're probably way ahead of me in getting the picture

of the parable of that fire-door system. Many churches have spiritual fire doors that close quickly when the flame of authentic Spirit-empowered renewal begins in some group. Some people fear the fire of the Spirit more than an actual conflagration of their church buildings. Much of the life of so many churches today is incombustible—our nonflammable traditions, our water-drenched procedures, and our icicle-laden lack of warmth and enthusiasm.

Fire Doors in Our Minds

But what's true of some churches today is also true of many church members. We have fire doors in our minds. Just as in a positive, protective way the fire doors of a building close when the alarm system is triggered, so too, in a negative, fearful way, the fire doors within us often close at the first signs of the Spirit's fire and power. We are afraid of what might happen to us if the Spirit surged through our whole being—if He entered into our minds, emotions, and wills—and through us into our relationships and attitudes.

Traditional religious people who desperately need the fire of the Spirit often respond with panic whenever the Spirit is emphasized, particularly in mainline denominational churches. They fear that it will lead to the introduction of the customs, clique words, and practices of groups focused on the Spirit.

Added to this there are fanatical "spiritites" who roam from church to church seeking to challenge pastors and congregations to be "Spirit-filled." Often they are very pushy in wanting their own brand of spiritual renewal. They are seldom satisfied. Their cries of "Fire, fire!" are often a false alarm that closes the spiritual fire doors in the minds of church members and leaders. Actually, it's the false replicas and the cheap substitutes of authentic Spirit-fire they are resisting.

But the closed door effect also is set off by an even deeper alarm system. Many of us are confused by who the Spirit is, how He works, and what it really means to be filled with His fire. Others of us wonder what might happen to us if we were taken hold of by the Spirit. Still others are content to live a self-sufficient life of trying to follow the message of Jesus on our own strength. And far too many of us are not attempting anything bold, adventuresome, and courageous enough to need the Spirit's wisdom and power, much less His fire.

One of the greatest needs among Christians and churches today is for an authentic experience and continued outpouring of the fire of the Spirit. It is impossible to live a dynamic Christian life without that fire. The fire doors in our minds not only shut out the blessings, but contradict the central purpose of the other Jesus.

Jesus' Ultimate Mission—Fire on the Earth

In one of the most challenging of His hard sayings, Jesus said, "I came to send fire on the earth, and how I wish it were already kindled! But I have a baptism to be baptized with, and how distressed I am until it is accomplished!" (Luke 12:49–50).

This hard saying presses us to enter into the other Jesus' inner heart, thoughts, and feelings about His ultimate mission. Our presuppositions about why He came into the world are stretched beyond our familiar understanding.

If you had to tell someone why Jesus came into the world, how would you put it? To reveal what God is like and what we were meant to be? Of course. To give us abundant life? Thankfully, yes. To explain the Kingdom of God and call us to it? Surely. To suffer and die for the sins of the world and reconcile us to God in the sacrifice of the cross? Indeed.

To conquer the power of death and give us victory through the resurrection? Sublimely so!

But as magnificent as all these blessings are, we have not reached beyond to grasp Jesus' ultimate goal. What else is needed? He makes that clear in this hard saying. He came to send fire on the earth.

It is important to understand what that fire is. Many have interpreted it as judgment and destruction. That would contradict Jesus' response to the disciples who, a few days before, had wanted to command a fire to come down from heaven and consume a Samaritan village that had rejected Jesus. He said, "You do not know what spirit you are of. For the Son of Man did not come to destroy men's lives but to save them" (Luke 9:55–56).

Jesus did warn His listeners about the fires of hell after death for those who rejected the kingdom. But only here in this hard saying does He talk about sending fire *on the earth*. And He puts it in terms of the reason for His coming. Again we ask, what is that fire He came to send on the earth?

We find our answer in the prophecy of John the Baptist and in the Spirit-filled believers described in the Book of Acts. John prophesied, "I indeed baptize you with water, but One mightier than I is coming, whose sandal strap I am not worthy to loose. He will baptize you with the Holy Spirit and with fire" (Luke 3:16). That's exactly what happened at Pentecost. And across the pages of Acts we witness the birth of a new humanity, new creatures in Christ, men and women filled and aflame with His Spirit.

Before the Fire—The Cross

This is what Jesus foresaw when He spoke the promise in the words of His hard saying about sending fire on the earth.

He saw a new creation of people who would abide in Him and in whom He would abide. How Jesus longed for that! No wonder He said, "How I wish it were already kindled!" But He knew that before that could happen He would have to go to the cross to die for the sins which kept people from the abundant and eternal life He came to make possible. Then He would rise from the dead in victorious defeat of Satan's power and the fear of death. This was the confidence Jesus had as He made His way to Jerusalem. His purpose would be accomplished!

Now we can empathize with the urgency Jesus expresses in the second half of this hard saying we're considering. "But I have a baptism to be baptized with, and how distressed I am till it is accomplished." Jesus was referring here to the cross. He knew that He would be immersed in the overwhelming afflictions of Calvary as He took upon Himself the sins of humankind—past, present, and future. Before the outpouring of His Spirit, the complete, once-for-all, never-to-be-repeated cosmic atonement had to be finished.

Jesus yearned to get on with it. Note that He said, "How distressed I am until it is accomplished." The English word "distressed" in the New King James Version hardly captures what He was feeling. The Greek word used to translate Jesus' original Aramaic word is *sunechomai*, meaning "held back, constrained, pressed in." He was feeling the constraint of being in the flesh in His earthly ministry. He longed to go through the pain and suffering of the cross and receive the vindication of the resurrection. Then, glorified by the Father, He would be loosed on the world as the ubiquitous, omnipresent Lord of the new creation He had come to establish. He knew that the love and forgiveness of His cross would transform men and women and that His resurrection would raise them out of the graves of doubt, fear, and reservation.

They would be ready for the fire He would set ablaze in their minds and hearts with His indwelling Spirit.

The Spreading Fire

This ties right in with what two followers of Christ experienced when they met Him on the Emmaus road shortly after the resurrection. They described their experience of the living Lord as a fire burning in their hearts. "Did not our hearts burn within us while He talked with us on the road, and while He opened the Scriptures to us?" (Luke 24:32). That was only the beginning of what was to happen when Christ's regenerating fire came upon and dwelt in the apostles as the church was born. And the fire spread as the new creatures of the new creation radiated the splendor of their blazing hearts.

One of the pivotal people who received the fire of Christ's Spirit and spread it throughout the then-known world was a Pharisee named Paul. He summarized the full sweep of the Fire-bringer's ministry as Jesus of Nazareth and as risen, indwelling Lord. "When the fullness of time had come, God sent forth His Son, born of a woman, born under the law, to redeem those who were under the law, that we might receive the adoption as sons. And because you are sons, God has sent forth the Spirit of His Son into your hearts, crying out, 'Abba! Father!' " (Gal. 4:4–6). The birthright of all Christians is the fire of Christ's indwelling Spirit.

"On Fire" Christians

That makes us wonder why there are so few "on fire" Christians today. Why do we have fire doors in our minds to shut off the spread of His fire within us and in our churches? Perhaps it is because we've never imagined what it might be like to be fully on fire. Like physical fire, Christ's Spirit purifies, refines, radiates from us, and brings warmth to others through us. And it all begins when we ask Him to set us aflame.

The fire begins in *our minds*. Christ works in us to prepare the kindling of a sensed need for Him. When we accept Him as Savior, a spark is lit and begins to grow to the full blaze of burning conviction. Jesus' cross becomes personal and powerful. We are released from the need for self-justification and know that we are loved and completely absolved of past sin and failure. The resurrection becomes real and we know that we are alive forever. Our thinking is purified. Memories are healed. The chaff of distorted ideas about ourselves and about life is burned up.

It is then that the refining process begins. Just as in the smelting of raw materials in which the impurities rise to the surface and are skimmed off, so too Christ's fire purges with red hot assurance that Christ is not only our Savior, but Sovereign Lord of all. The result of the refining is that our thinking brain is filled with the mind of Christ. He is able to think His thoughts through us. That profoundly affects our attitudes. We see people differently. Our vision of the future is filled with hope and excitement.

Next, the fire of Christ in our minds spreads to *our wills*. The hardness of our volitional resistance is melted by the warmth of His flaming Spirit. We begin to want His will above all else. Our longing is to have our personalities remolded into His image. We want His guidance in every decision; our minds are gripped by a burning desire. That's a miracle. As G. K. Chesterton put it:

> In a time of skeptic moths and cynic rusts
> And fatted lives that of their sweetness tire,
> In a world of flying loves and fading lusts,
> It is something to be sure of a desire.[1]

And the desire of a fire-filled person is to live fully for Christ. That desire drives us to prayer at the beginning and end of each day and in all the intervening hours. The fire of Christ burns out our reluctance and in its place produces a resiliency. We are anxious to know more about Him and to do what He wants. Instead of engaging in a tug-of-war with the Master, we are pulled on by the desire to experience serendipities of His grace—surprises we would not have imagined He had waiting for us.

With the fire door of the will wide open, the fire of Christ's Spirit surges into *our emotions*. Here again a refining takes place. Old patterns of emotional reaction to life and people are purified. Whatever hurts we have nursed over the years with misspent emotion are burned away. In the warmth of Christ's fire of unqualified love, we feel loved in spite of the rejections or misunderstandings we have endured. We become free to feel accepted and cherished.

The Fire of Love

The result is that we are liberated to express profound love. Our words, actions, and touch are released from bondage to express tenderness, forgiveness, and assurance to others. A cold Christian is a contradiction of terms. Coldness or even aloof coolness is simply an outward sign of the absence of Christ's fire.

When Christ's fire does burn in us, a new verve and vitality is expressed in all we do. We become cheerleaders for others

---

1. "The Great Minimum," stanza v.

and tackle tasks with an assurance of unlimited spiritual power to see us through. People with Christ's fire burning in their hearts are fun to live with. Their radiance lights up the dullness of life's routines.

The fire of Christ's love is the secret of their effectiveness in communicating their faith to others. They don't need slick evangelism brochures or constant guilt-producing challenges from their pastors to reach out to others. Reaching out comes naturally, and therefore is winsome. Because they care profoundly, they want everyone to know the Lord and receive His Spirit. But instead of being firebrands, they are people who are branded with the fire of Christ's character and compassion. And that leads them into both social responsibility and personal involvement with people who need the Lord.

The Church on Fire

What happens to a church when its membership is filled with authentic, "on-fire" Christians? It becomes a loving and forgiving fellowship. Worship is alive with praise and joy. There are no fire doors around the pulpit to confine the blaze of the Spirit burning in the exposition of the Bible. It spreads to the pews and out into all the classes and groups of the church. The leadership of the church becomes an incendiary force rather than a society of spiritual fire-fighters. The church as a whole becomes a warm fire to attract others. Acceptance and inclusiveness abounds. When visitors gather around the fire, the dry kindling of their own hearts is set afire.

Is this too much to expect from our churches today? Not at all! But we must remember that it is Christ and not we who sends fire. So many people who long for spiritual fire in the church take matters into their own hands. As I mentioned earlier, they think that a transformation can be pulled off by the introduction of practices and customs that identify churches claiming to be filled with the Spirit. Let's keep in mind that it's His miracle, not our manipulation, that brings the real fire.

How Churches Are Set on Fire

How then are Christians and churches set on fire? What changes the spiritual fire doors so that they open rather than close when Christ desires to send the fire of His Spirit?

The secret is in this hard saying of the other Jesus. From it we are assured that it is His continuing purpose to give the fire. He longs for it to be kindled. But just as He had to go to the cross before that purpose could be realized, so too there is a cross that stands between us and authentic spiritual fire. That cross requires us to die to self and place our complete trust in Him.

We must give up our clever schemes of manipulated revival. Only then, when we are empty of our own plans and demands, will the fire descend. And before His infilling is outwardly evident, His refining work must be done inwardly.

People will observe the inner fire and feel the warmth of the flames of love leaping within us. Others in whom the same fire is burning will be galvanized with us in praying for the Spirit's fire to spread throughout the congregation as a whole.

Our prayer will be, "Lord, we need the fire; we want the fire; we surrender our lives completely to receive the fire!"

Christ came, and comes, to set fire on the earth. He went through the baptism of the cross to prepare the kindling of our minds and hearts so that He might baptize us with fire. What he has done in ready, kindled minds and hearts through the centuries, He is prepared and willing to do today. And if we are not on fire with His indwelling Spirit, we are missing not only His declared purpose, but also the burning conviction, purified desire, warm love and enthusiasm, and the radiant inner glow He wants for all of us.

The fire of Christ's Spirit is not an optional addition to salvation and eternal life; it is the gift that makes both of those a flaming assurance that nothing can extinguish. A favorite poem, whose author is unknown to me, contains a beautiful plea for forgiveness of the cowardice and fears that have stifled the fire of love within us over the years. Its last lines read,

> Fire of love, burn in us, burn evermore
> Till we burn out for Thee.

I'd like to suggest a different line to close that poem. With Christ's fire aflame in us, we will not burn out. Rather, this:

> Fire of love, burn in us, burn evermore,
> Now and for eternity.

CHAPTER EIGHT

Assuredly, I say to you, all sins will be forgiven the sons of men, and whatever blasphemies they may utter; but he who blasphemes against the Holy Spirit never has forgiveness, but is subject to eternal condemnation. . . .
(Mark 3:28–29)

THE ONE SIN GOD CAN'T FORGIVE

===

"I've committed the unforgivable sin!" the young woman sobbed as she confessed to having an affair with a married man.

"What makes you think that what you've done is unforgivable?" I asked.

"It's what I've always been taught," she said, wiping away the tears streaming down her face. "Ever since I was a young girl, my parents warned me about the sin of sex before marriage. And when I started seeing this married man, they became livid. 'If you get into trouble with that guy,' they said repeatedly, 'don't expect us to forgive you! And don't go running to *God*—He won't forgive you either.' "

"Are you sorry for what you've done and willing to break off your relationship with this man?" I asked tenderly. "If you are and I could prove to you that God does forgive adultery when it is confessed, would you want to receive His forgiveness?"

"Oh, yes!" she cried, her face brightening with hope.

In the hour that followed, I told her about the loving, forgiving heart of God revealed in Christ and about the atonement of the cross. We reviewed passages in the New Testament in which Christ dealt with people who confessed their sin.

Though the young woman had been in a youth group in her church in the Midwest and had been confirmed, her experience of Christ's love had been conditioned by her parents' qualified teaching of His forgiveness. By the end of our hour together she met Christ personally and had a profound experience of His pardon.

So many times during my ministry, I've talked with people who confessed what they thought was an unforgivable sin. It's usually the sin they'd considered the most serious, the one they had promised themselves they would never commit. But the very fact that they realized their sin and wanted it to be forgiven clearly indicated that it was not an unpardonable one.

Is "Can't" Too Strong a Word?

Is there a sin God can't forgive? Yes, as the title of this chapter affirms, I believe there is an unforgivable sin.

"Doesn't the word 'can't' limit God?" you ask. "Don't we believe God can do anything He wants to do? Wouldn't it be better to say that there may be a sin God 'won't' forgive? Aren't you limiting His sovereign power?"

Let the word "can't" stand for a moment. Before you decide whether I have contradicted God's unqualified love and unconditional forgiveness, let's consider one of the most disturbing and misunderstood of the hard sayings of the other Jesus. "Assuredly, I say to you, all sins will be forgiven the sons of men, and whatever blasphemies they may utter; but he who blasphemes against the Holy Spirit never has forgiveness, but is subject to eternal condemnation" (Mark 3:28–29).

This saying about what has been called the unforgivable sin has distressed people through the ages. Halford Luccock wrote, "If, with reverence, a list of the sayings of Jesus were assembled under the heading of 'the things I wish Jesus never had said,' this would rank high among them. This word on the 'unforgivable sin' has had a strange fascination and terror for many minds. The distorting of it has filled insane asylums with minds broken down by a guilt complex . . . yet the context makes the meaning clear and simple." [1]

What Prompted This Hard Saying?

Dr. Luccock was right; the context does reveal what prompted Jesus' hard saying. When we understand the circumstances in which He made it, we begin to understand.

The news that Jesus was casting out demons had reached Jerusalem. A delegation of scribes was sent to investigate, but the highly trained legalists in the interpretation of the law had already come to a firm judgment before they talked to Jesus. Because they did not accept his claim to be the Messiah, some other explanation had to be made of His power over demons. "He has Beelzebub," they concluded. "By the ruler of demons he casts out demons."

The name Beelzebub in Hebrew means "Baal the prince." This had been the title of the chief god of Ekron. Also, in

---

1. *Matthew, Mark*, The Interpreter's Bible, 8 vols. (Nashville, TN: Abingdon-Cokesbury Press, 1951) 7:693.

the conquest of the Promised Land, the Israelites had confronted the Canaanites' worship of Baal, a fertility god. At the time of Jesus' ministry, Beelzebub was designated as the chief of demons in Jewish demonology. Another name for him was Satan. By whatever name, he was considered to be the power of evil in command of the host of demons.

The Incisive Other Jesus

Jesus' response to the charge that it was by Beelzebub's power that He was casting out demons was magnificently logical and incisive. "How can Satan cast out Satan? If a kingdom is divided against itself, that kingdom cannot stand. And if a house is divided against itself, that house cannot stand. And if Satan has risen up against himself, and is divided, he cannot stand, but has an end. No one can enter a strong man's house and plunder his goods, unless he first binds the strong man and then he will plunder his house" (Mark 3:23–27).

The Master's very striking argument was that Satan would not destroy his own kingdom, and that's just what would be happening if Jesus was casting out demons by means of Satan's power. Rather, when Jesus exorcised demons from people He was plundering Satan's demonic possession. The only way He could have done that was by a power greater than Satan. But, throughout His ministry, Jesus clearly stated that it was by the Spirit of God that He cast out demons. In other words, the scribes were not only questioning His authority, but also the power of the Spirit at work in and through Him. These legalists from Jerusalem were blaspheming. The word "blaspheme" means to "insult, show contempt, fail to reverence, or to engage in defamatory or contemptuous speech against God or sacred things." The Spirit of God was incarnate, alive, in Jesus and also was actively seeking to convince people that the Master was the long-awaited Messiah. So the scribes were not only blasting Jesus but were showing contempt for God!

The Unforgivable Sin

That's what motivated Jesus' hard saying about the unforgivable sin. All blasphemies could be forgiven except one: the blasphemy against the Holy Spirit. That blasphemy was to deny the one thing the Spirit was seeking to do in the scribes—confirm in their minds and hearts that Jesus was the divine Son of God. Mark goes on to clarify their denial: "Because they said, 'He has an unclean spirit'" (3:30). That is, they were deliberately attributing to Satan what Christ, by His own testimony, had done through the power of the Spirit of God. And the Greek word Mark used here for "said" suggests that the scribes said it not once, but continually.

It was this willful commitment to blindness that Jesus condemned. That is stressed even more pointedly in Matthew's version of the Master's saying about the unforgivable sin. "Therefore, I say to you, every sin and blasphemy will be forgiven men, but the blasphemy against the Spirit will not be forgiven men. Anyone who speaks against the Son of Man, it will be forgiven him; but whoever speaks against the Holy Spirit, it will not be forgiven him, either in this age or the age to come" (Matt. 12:31–32).

During the course of Jesus' ministry, many found the cost of discipleship too high. Others were threatened by His exposure of their prejudices, selfishness, and lack of love. These people often criticized Jesus and His message. But they were not guilty of the unforgivable sin. It was true they were in perilous danger, but the door of opportunity had not yet been closed completely. There was a hardness forming, but it was not yet firmly set. Jesus' cross and resurrection would soften that hardness in many of them, and through the Spirit's power some would claim Him as Lord and Savior.

Many of the scribes, however, were not only resisting the Spirit of God in His efforts to convince them that Jesus was truly the Divine Messiah. They had also taken the fateful step into the netherworld of calling evil what was good. There could be no question that the people Jesus had exorcised had been liberated and healed. To attribute that mercy and grace to Satan was to overturn all the Jews had believed about God and His gracious Providence through the centuries. It was like praising Satan for the sunrise, the beauty of the natural world, and their sacred law and heritage. Even though they knew that nothing except the power of God could exorcise demons, the scribes would not recognize God's Spirit at work in the Messiah during His ministry and they would refuse to receive His atoning death for their sins on Calvary.

Here's the point. Their sin was unpardonable because it was never confessed. They could not say, "O Lord, be merciful to me a sinner." Only a sinner needs a savior. And the scribes truly denied that need. That denial didn't happen suddenly. Many rejections of the promptings of the Spirit, multiplied by the scribes' willfulness, finally equalled the spiritual and psychological condition beyond the reach of pardon.

Four Ways of Resisting the Spirit

You're probably wondering what all this has to do with the one sin I've claimed that God can't forgive today. I am by no means suggesting that people in the twentieth century would commit the sin of saying that Christ's power is demonic. But many resist the influence of the power of His Spirit today.

The sin against the Spirit is committed by four groups of people today.

The first group is made up of those who refuse the Spirit's inspiration to recognize and confess their spiritual emptiness. Like the scribes, they seal their eternal doom. They insulate themselves against admitting their need. Sin is separation from the Lord, independence, missing the mark of the target of why we are born. In millions of people today, there is no confession and therefore there can be no forgiveness. In attitude, if not in word, the theme song of these self-complacent people is:

> I fight alone and win or sink,
> I need no one to make me free,
> I want no Jesus Christ to think
> That He could ever die for me.

But there's *a second group* of people who may be in danger of the unforgivable sin. These are people who claim that they are Christians, but insist on self-justification as their only means of handling their failures and inadequacies. They blame others, life, or circumstances for their difficulties. Or they cover their sins by trying harder to be adequate. Some use the oblation of hard work, self-improvement, plans, or the sharp edge of self-criticism to atone for themselves. Anything's better than the honest confession, "Lord, I've failed and made a mess of things. Forgive me and fill me with Your power to do Your will and be the person You meant me to be." Again, without confession there is no realization of the forgiveness the Lord offers.

The third group includes those who resist claiming Christ as the source of their strength for the challenges of life. He is constantly nudging us to accept His power and guidance.

Most everyday inspiration comes with specific marching orders. We are called to love difficult people, to forgive when forgiveness isn't deserved on our terms, to become involved with those who desperately need hope and encouragement.

The first "no" to the Lord's Spirit is a traumatic refusal. Then it becomes easier. Finally, our whole life becomes closed to an intimate fellowship with Him. Prayer becomes routine and then infrequent. Bible study is neglected, and dependence on the Lord is inconsistent, and then disappears. On a daily, practical level we say "no" so often and so long that it becomes impossible for us to say "yes." We become insensitive to the ministry of the Spirit who seeks to press us into greatness. Self-satisfaction and mediocrity set in. Again, no confession, no forgiveness.

Paul speaks of the ministry of the Spirit in very personal terms: "Do not grieve the Holy Spirit of God" (Eph. 4:30). The Christian life is not a set of rules to be followed, but a personal relationship with the Lord. The fire of the Spirit we talked about in the previous chapter can be banked and in time will flicker out if it isn't fueled with the fresh kindling of willingness to do the Lord's will. Paul's challenge to the Thessalonians is, "Do not quench the Spirit" (1 Thess. 5:19). He means—don't put out the fire.

Earlier, Paul told his Thessalonian readers, "Rejoice always, pray without ceasing, in everything give thanks; for this is the will of God in Christ Jesus for you" (1 Thess. 5:16–18). That means living life as a privilege, wide open to thank the Lord for all that He's doing in both the difficulties and delights of our lives. When we neglect that quality of praise, we begin to feel victimized by the people and problems that upset us. It isn't long before we have a negative feeling that we have to grind out each day with grim determination and self-generated effort. When we resist the praise-inducing ministry of the Spirit, we are on the way to closing ourselves to His intervening power. That, too, is sin against the Lord's Spirit.

We then become candidates for *the fourth group* of people who often believe more in Satan's power than in Christ's. That's what happened to the scribes. They were more convinced of Beelzebub's power than they were able to recognize the Spirit's power working in Jesus. The resistance to the Spirit created a vacuum in them which was filled by Satan's influence.

For us that results in spiritual insensitivity and moral obtuseness. An immense negativism produces a pervading depression. We can actually become an agent of evil by resisting the good. We become vulnerable to say and do what cripples the progress of the Lord's plan for us. We hurt and weaken others. After awhile we don't even know we are working against the Lord. We think there is nothing to confess because we have been lulled into the false sense of self-righteousness. God does not refuse to forgive, but we have refused the impulse of the Spirit to ask.

And the result? We move closer to believing that we no longer need or want forgiveness. The word for "forgive" in Greek is *aphiēmi*, "to send away." *Apo*–"from"; *hiēmi*–"send." The Lord can't send away from us something we've convinced ourselves we haven't committed!

The Recognition of Our Need

Wherever among the above groups we might find ourselves, we are in danger of committing the unforgivable sin. Bishop Fulton J. Sheen, in a lecture I heard him give at Princeton Theological Seminary, put it this way: "The really unforgivable sin is the denial of sin, because, by its very nature, there is now nothing to be forgiven." There is no pardon because there is no recognition of the need of it or desire for it.

The apostle John describes this condition in vivid terms. "If we say that we have no sin, we deceive ourselves, and the truth is not in us. If we confess our sins, He is faithful and just to forgive us our sins and to cleanse us from all unrighteousness. If we say that we have not sinned, we make Him a liar, and His word is not in us" (1 John 1:8–10).

Now I hope you see why I've used the word "can't" in the title of this chapter. The one sin God can't forgive is whatever sin we refuse to confess. And the danger is that that one sin becomes many. When we refuse the Spirit's effort to create in us a sense of need, to bring us to the cross, and to assure us of complete forgiveness, we imprison ourselves in our own jails of excuses, self-incriminations and eventual denials of any failure. Whittier describes that condition:

> What if thine eye refuse to see,
> Thine ear of Heaven's free welcome fail,
> And thou a willing captive be,
> Thyself thy own dark jail? [1]

The Demarcation Line

Your mind has probably leaped ahead with mine to the eternal ramifications of what we've been discussing throughout this chapter. It is frightening to consider the consequences of deliberately rejecting the overtures of God's love and losing the desire for pardon and eventually the ability to receive it. The other Jesus clearly said that we would be subject to an eternal separation from God.

There seems to be an invisible demarcation line to which we move closer with each refusal. On the other side of that

---

1. "The answer," stanza xv.

line is a hardened heart no longer open to the influence of the Spirit. I've known Christians who, step by step, move closer to that line. And I've known others who seem to have crossed over. They no longer want the Lord or His loving forgiveness. You and I may be a long way from that line, but we need to question: Have I stepped toward it or away from it today?

As long as we are alive physically, the Lord does not relent in His efforts to reach us. He wants us to know the joy of heaven now. Then our physical death will be a release to greater freedom to enjoy Him forever.

What If?

And if we reject the Lord until we no longer want Him? What if all the little unconfessed sins add up to the ultimate unconfessed sin of no longer desiring His grace? He will not deny the freedom of choice He has given us. Our sin will be unforgiven and all eternity will be spent in the anguish of the joy we missed!

Now, let me reword the title of this chapter: There's no sin God can't forgive—if we confess it.

CHAPTER NINE

And forgive us our sins, for we also forgive everyone who is indebted to us. And do not lead us into temptation, but deliver us from the evil one.

(Luke 11:4)

THE TEST OF LOVE

Understanding some of the hard sayings of Jesus is like going swimming in the ocean when the surf is high. First, we must stand knee-high in the foaming sea of popular interpretations of these hard sayings. Then we are ready to wade out and brave the waves of a more challenging explanation. Finally, we are prepared to plunge into the depths of the deeper, more profound truths of what Jesus really meant.

You may be surprised when I tell you what the hard saying is that I think needs that kind of three-phase reflection. It is the familiar petition from the Lord's prayer, "Lead us not into temptation, but deliver us from the evil one" (Luke 11:4).

Questions in the Shallows

While we are still in the shallows, we wonder, "Would a good God ever lead us into temptation? If not, why would the other Jesus teach us to pray this petition?" That is a difficult question for many people.

Over brunch one Sunday after church, a conversation with my friend Bob suddenly shifted from general pleasantries to a profound discussion that lasted late into the afternoon. This petition from the Lord's Prayer was on Bob's mind and he wanted to talk about it.

"I've repeated the Lord's Prayer ever since I was a little boy," Bob said thoughtfully. "This morning in the worship service as we prayed it together, I found it difficult to say the words 'Lead us not into temptation.' Lately I've been thinking a lot about that. I can't imagine that God would ever deliberately lead me into temptation. So why pray that He won't?

"Frankly," Bob went on, "I've got enough temptations to battle with as it is. The idea that God might lead me into more and that I have to beg Him not to with this line from the Lord's Prayer really has me confused. I guess I've missed the point. But whatever the answer is—I'm not going to pray that part of the Lord's Prayer again until I'm sure."

A Popular Answer

How would you have responded to Bob? In a surface interpretation, many of us would suggest a popular understanding of the petition. We'd tell Bob that it really means "Keep us from temptation and subdue the evil one who constantly tries to lure us into temptation."

And we'd be right—at least for openers. We're tempted

all the time and we need the Lord to protect us from evil influence. We are really asking that He intervene to keep us out of relationships with people who would lead us astray and out of situations in which our faith might be compromised.

To fortify our interpretation of Jesus' hard saying, we might underline some biblical cross-references that have become a source of courage for us in our battles with temptation. We'd probably turn to James 1:13 as a strong reaffirmation that God does not tempt us. "Let no one say when he is tempted, 'I am tempted by God'; for God cannot be tempted by evil, nor does He Himself tempt anyone."

And when we've been under the pressure of some temptation, we've felt a special surge of strength from Paul's reassurance of God's faithfulness. "No temptation has overtaken you except such as is common to man; but God is faithful, who will not allow you to be tempted beyond what you are able, but with the temptation will also make the way of escape, that you may be able to bear it" (1 Cor. 10:13).

All of us could give specific examples from our own lives of how God has blocked us from pressing on with some selfish desire that would hurt us or someone else. Who could make it through any week—any day for that matter—without the ways of escape that He provides to keep us from saying or doing what might destroy us?

God makes us uncomfortable with "white lies" that may become a pattern of dishonesty. Before we step over the line and damage or destroy someone's character, He confronts us with our demeaning attitudes and cutting words of gossip. When we titillate our sexual needs by flirtation that could lead to sexual sins, He blocks us before we go too far. And think of the many times when He has made it impossible to go ahead with unguided decisions that would have led us away from Him and His plans for us.

Thank God that in His infinite wisdom and direct involvement in our lives He does close doors, put up roadblocks, and actively hinder us from doing what is not His best for us. And what's more, when we do fail, the Lord helps us deal with the temptation to condemn ourselves. The evil one lurks waiting for those times. The one thing he tries to keep us from doing is confessing our failure, receiving forgiveness, and making a new beginning. But Christ our Savior and Friend is more powerful than Satan. He gives us strength to overcome the temptation to become immobilized with self-condemnation.

So, on the basis of this first level of understanding, we pray, "Lord, you know how weak I am at times and how beguiling the evil one continues to be. Keep me out of the clutches of temptation!" That's a needed daily prayer, and our Lord answers in wondrous ways beyond our deserving or expectation. But that's not all Jesus intended in this hard saying.

Moving Deeper

We move out into deeper water when we understand that the Greek word for "temptation" (*peirasmon*) in this petition can also be translated as "trial." So in this context, the petition could be worded, "Lead us not into trial, but keep us from the evil one."

We've all known our share of trying times. They occur when our patience, strength, or endurance is stretched to the breaking point. People disappoint us, sickness invades our agenda, grief over the loss of loved ones engulfs us, or suddenly a reversal dashes our hopes and dreams. Remembering these soul-wracking times, we depend on the Lord to keep us free from trials of adversity.

Once again, we can't imagine that our loving Father would intentionally send trying times. We hold tenaciously onto our conviction that He does not send difficulties. Rather, we bring many of our problems on ourselves. Other problems may come from the people around us. And Satan always has his arsenal loaded with the diabolical ammunition of suffering. No, we say, God does not lead us into trials; but He may use them to help us grow as people.

As we look back over our difficult times, we affirm that we could not have made it through them without the Lord's help. We say with the psalmist, "I would have lost heart, unless I had believed / That I would see the goodness of the Lord / In the land of the living" (Ps. 27:13). And so we remind ourselves and others, "Wait on the Lord; / Be of good courage, / And He shall strengthen your heart; / Wait, I say, on the Lord!" (Ps. 27:14).

At this point in our discussion over brunch, my friend Bob expressed appreciation for the reassurance of my explanation of how God helps us in both temptations and trials. "But," he interjected, "you still have not dealt with that confusing 'lead us not' aspect of the petition." Then I told Bob I had kept that as a part of the big plunge into the deep.

The Big Plunge

The words "lead us not" really mean "bring us not." Any authentic explanation of what this petition means must include that idea. The Lord can and will bring us into whatever He considers necessary to keep us open and receptive to Him as Lord of our lives.

H. H. Farmer, in *The World and God*, said, "God our Father is absolute demand and absolute succor." We are accustomed to hearing more about the succor, His gracious love. But His demands also are a part of His love. As our Father, He does set standards, and He makes us very uncomfortable when we swagger with pride and assumed self-sufficiency. He is more than a co-pilot to help us reach *our* destinations. While we limit our goals to less than His vision for us, His purpose is so much more than simply being our self-esteem builder. And He's more than a "buddy" to keep us company as we saunter along life's road. He is sublimely our Friend, but only after we know Him as our Lord who demands absolute obedience.

An agnostic friend of mine in the movie business enjoys poking fun at Christians who think they have God in their hip pocket. The other day, he greeted me in what he thought was a clever way.

"Hi, Lloyd! How are you, and how is your cousin God?" I stopped dead in my tracks. I couldn't let that flip remark go by without some comment.

"God is not my cousin," I said in all seriousness. "He is my Father, loving Lord of my life." I went on to tell him what the Lord means to me.

My friend got more than he expected, and he was sorry that he had been so insensitive in his remark. Then he said, "You really believe that, don't you? God is not that real to me. I enjoy pricking the bubbles of overly pious Christians. I guess it's because I'd like to find God myself. Maybe we can talk someday about all this."

That conversation led to some good visits. After a few times together, I saw him one day at a studio where he was filming. "Hi, Lloyd," he said warmly. "How are you and how's your Father?" I smiled and responded, "We're both fine, and we both care about you very much!" The man's on the way; it won't be long before we'll be brothers in the Father's family.

My friend's flip remark about "cousin" God expresses the mood of our times. Even among Christians, He's been whittled down to our size. Awe and wonder are lacking. We've done our best to create a God who helps us but does not question our values or priorities. We talk to Him when we're in need, but deny His authority over our lives.

Christians today desperately need the Father. The other Jesus came to reveal His loving heart. But the limitless love of the Father that He communicated was not sentimental and coddling. That's why I think He included the words "Lead us not into temptation." But the word temptation also means "test." That's what I think Jesus meant. The *New English Bible* correctly translates this hard saying, "And do not bring us to the test, but save us from the evil one."

That caught Bob's attention. "Do we really believe that God tests us?" he asked urgently.

"Yes, Bob, I think He does; and if we've ever known one of those times of testing, we are more than ready to pray, 'Do not bring us to the test.'"

The Test

Now, a test is whatever exposes the real nature of something. In the laboratory we test a substance to determine its component parts. Metals are tested for their strength and durability. A car is road-tested to evaluate its safety.

I believe God tests us not because He wants to expose our weaknesses, but to introduce us to our real selves. The test is for us, not for Him.

Think of it this way. When we drift from the Lord and begin to run our own lives and resist the nudges and urgings of His Spirit, we are on a collision course with disaster. But graciously, He steps into the path of our speeding lives to stop us. So, the test is whatever means He uses to wake us up to where we are heading—to expose us to our real destination—before it's too late. When we seek independence from accountability to Him, something has to be done.

Sometimes the Lord may test us by using the tragedies that happen in our lives to alert us to how far we have wandered from Him. Sickness and pain can be megaphone warnings from Him. The dark night of the soul can make us long again for the dawn of His love.

I'm not suggesting, though, that all of life's difficulties are a test. For a person who is open and receptive to the Lord's love and guidance, problems become an occasion for deepening the relationship with Him. But for the person whose relationship with the Lord has become progessively distant until it hardly exists at all—the test is a shocking realization of what he or she has allowed to happen over the years of neglect or blatant rebellion.

This hard saying / petition, "Do not bring us to the test," is really Jesus' potent antidote to help build up our spiritual immune system against the unforgivable sin we talked about in the previous chapter. Praying this petition is a daily vaccination to prevent the necessity for God's having to test us.

Now we are ready for the hardest question of all. Would it be love to allow us to drift until we no longer sense our need or desire for the Lord? Hardly.

Think of David. He'd been called a "man after God's own heart." And yet, he failed miserably in that when he committed adultery with Bathsheba and arranged for her husband's death. But God did not allow the King to be engulfed in his remorse. Instead, he sent Nathan to confront David with what he had done. And the Lord didn't give up on David until he confessed.

In David's prayer of repentance he clearly identified his brokenness as a gift of God. "Make me to hear joy and gladness, / That the bones which You have broken may rejoice. / Hide Your face from my sins, / And blot out all my iniquities. / Create in me a clean heart, O God, / And renew a steadfast spirit within me. / Do not cast me away from Your presence, / And take not Your Holy Spirit from me" (Ps. 51:8–11).

Don't miss the words "the bones which You have broken." The test of the Lord often does that. It breaks our willful efforts to explain away what we've done or what has been done to us.

Several present-day examples of how the Lord brings us to the test come to my mind. I think of Lisa and Hugh. During Hugh's prolonged illness, he and Lisa rediscovered the Lord and each other. Hugh said reflectively, "I'm sure sorry it took this scrape with death to wake us up to what we've been missing. When our comfortable life fell apart, we were forced to see how empty our lives and our marriage had become. I hope I'll never have to go through something as radical as this again, but I wouldn't trade what it has taught us for a million dollars!"

Then, there is Susie, who had become progressively hardened to God's love. When she was divorced, she blamed her husband. When she lost her job, she faulted the man for whom she had worked. When her friends didn't measure up to her expectations, she complained that no one cared.

But when Susie's son, her pride and joy, stole a car and was put into jail, she cried out for God's help. I remember her prayer. "Lord, I've almost completely forgotten You. It's hard to imagine that I could have done that, remembering how much You meant to me years ago. Now nothing is working right. And for the first time, I see myself for what I am— someone who desperately needs You!"

Susie had taken the first step back to the Lord. The test had reintroduced her to her real self and once again to the Lord who was waiting with outstretched arms. And then she was ready to accept His help in straightening out her son's problems.

When I think of how God does put us to the test before it's too late, Jerry also comes to mind. I had known Jerry during his seminary days here in the Los Angeles area. Of all of the seminarians I have known, few had shown more promise than Jerry. After seminary, he became the pastor of a church in the Midwest. He threw himself into the duties of building up the membership, starting a building program and working with people night and day. Soon his quiet time each day with the Lord was set aside to meet his busy schedule. Eventually, he hardly prayed at all, except as a part of his public pastoral duties. He did Bible study only to get ready to preach, seldom for the enrichment of his own spiritual life.

Then about four years or so into his ministry, Jerry began to act strangely. He became autocratic, hostile, and angry. Soon his marriage was in trouble. The officers of his church warned him that his attitude was crippling his ministry. The forward movement of the church ground to a halt. Jerry blamed the resistance of his people. One day, he left.

Jerry had had it with the ministry. Not knowing where he was headed, he got into his car and began driving west. Three weeks later, Jerry arrived in Los Angeles. The lonely drive over the mountains and down to the coast had been a traumatic experience. But the Lord had been with him and confronted him with his four-year drift from Him. By the time he reached me, he was ready to take a long, hard look at himself.

Fortunately, Jerry didn't try to put the blame on his wife, the difficult religious traditionalists in his church, or the demands of his schedule. He realized that he had tried to live on his own strength and talents rather than on God's power.

And whether or not he ever had a chance to serve as a clergy-man again, he wanted the joy and peace he'd known before he had closed God out of his life.

After several visits, Jerry was ready to go home and face whatever happened. The Lord stepped in to pull off a miracle. Both his wife and his church welcomed Jerry back. He now sees that only God could have made that possible. This is what he wrote me.

> I'm sure the Lord had been trying to get through to me for a long time. He didn't have to wait until I almost lost my family and my church. It was I who held Him at arm's length. The near nervous breakdown I went through was not His doing, but my own. The wonder of it all is that He didn't let me crash completely. He let the boil fester until it came to a head, and then He lanced it with His judgment and healed it with His grace. My great regret is that I fought against His healing for so long. Now I pray constantly that I'll not make that kind of a heartbreaking encounter with the Lord necessary again.

Unfortunately, I also remember people whose lives have fallen apart and who even then have resisted the Lord's help. "What did I do to deserve this?" they wonder, rather than asking, "What is the Lord seeking to tell me in this?" The Lord's efforts to reach them in their difficulties are rebuffed. Bitterness sets in, and God is made the enemy.

Deliver Us from the Evil One

Behind that attitude is the clever work of the evil one. Satan wants to keep us from an intimate relationship with the Lord at all costs. He tries to influence us to doubt, to feel fear, and to enjoy self-pity. This is like spreading kerosene in our souls where he can ignite it with his temptations. Satan wants to get us to the place where we feel like helpless victims. The last thing he wants for us to do is thank the Lord for waking us up to reality, commit our problems to Him, and return to a relationship of confident trust in Him.

This is why praying the second half of this petition, "Deliver us from the evil one," is so crucial. Christ went to the cross and rose from the dead to answer this petition. So we pray it looking back to what He has done for us and forward to what He will do. On the cross, Christ confronted Satan and won. Now Satan cowers in the presence of Christ and flees at the mention of His powerful Name.

Christ the Deliverer

Christ has delivered us and does deliver us. The word "deliver" in this petition means both to "rescue from" and to "preserve from." In other words, Christ has rescued us from Satan's stranglehold on our lives, and He preserves us from his influence on our daily thinking and attitudes.

In another of Jesus' hard sayings, He tells us that we have authority over Satan. "I give you authority to trample on serpents and scorpions, and over all the power of the enemy, and nothing shall by any means hurt you. Nevertheless, do not rejoice in this, that the spirits are subject to you, but rather rejoice because your names are written in heaven" (Luke 10:18–20).

In the time when Jesus first spoke this promise, the phrase "serpents and scorpions" commonly denoted evil. Imagine, He said that we can trample on evil! We do that when we claim Christ's authority and power over Satan. When he tries to tempt us with doubt or discouragement, we can say, "Satan, in the Name of Christ who defeated you on the cross, you have no power over me. I belong to Christ—now get out of my way!" We belong to the Lord. Filled with His Spirit, we do have His authority over evil.

So when we pray, "Deliver us from the evil one," we are not praying a passive petition. Rather, we are claiming that we are co-warriors with Christ. We have been recruited to pray in His Name to overcome Satan's influence on us, other people, and situations.

Claiming the authority given us is a sure defense against our ever drifting into the place where the Lord would have to bring us to the test to convince us of how much He loves us and how much we love Him. We no longer overestimate Satan's influence to tempt us to think that we can run our own lives. But even better, we no longer underestimate Christ's power to defeat Satan's strategies.

A Victorious Prayer

With our new understanding of this hard saying / petition we can now honestly say, "Lord, help me to live in such close communion with You, open to Your guidance and willing to obey, that You do not have to bring me to the test of my love for You. Thank You for rescuing me from Satan's power and from his beguiling influence."

What I've written in this chapter is essentially what I shared with my friend Bob that Sunday afternoon during and after brunch. Bob sat silently for a long time after our discussion. Then he spoke with intensity.

"Lloyd, I'm overcome with how much God loves us. That's what I'm going to think about when I pray this part of the Lord's Prayer. Thanks for the plunge into the deep!"

CHAPTER TEN

Hypocrites! You know how to discern the face of the sky, but you cannot discern the signs of the times.
(Matthew 16:3)

IT'S ABOUT TIME!

Horace Whittel, a dock worker in Gillingham, England, hated his alarm clock. Every working day for forty-seven years, its bell had jarred him awake. Each day he had longed to ignore it.

Finally Whittel got his revenge. On the day he retired, he took his alarm clock to the dockyards. He placed it under an 80-ton hydraulic press. Then with great delight, he pushed the button releasing the press down on the clock. It was totally flattened. "What a lovely feeling!" Whittel said.

Many of us can empathize. We have a love-hate relationship with alarm clocks, watches, and timepieces. But even if we were to spend the rest of our lives destroying them to express our exasperation with the pressure of time, we'd not escape the persistent swing of the pendulum or the tick of the clock or the quartz movements of registered time.

We tend to speak of time in very concrete, sometimes personal terms. We say we have "time on our hands" or ask, "Do you have the time?" We talk about using time, saving it, wasting it, killing it, or making it up. And some who have committed a crime must "do" time. Yet, we all would have difficulty defining time.

Saint Augustine said, "What is time? If someone asks me I know. If I wish to explain it to someone who asks, I know not." We'd agree. And even after a thorough study of the history of the measurement of time, we still find it difficult to define what it is. We feel its movement; we are frustrated when we have too little of it or too much to do in an allotted amount of it. My friend R. Alex Mackenzie, author of *The Time Trap*, says, "No one has enough time, yet everyone has all there is."

If we sleep eight hours of the 24 hours of every day, that means we have 16 hours for wide-awake use of time. That's 960 momentous minutes and 57,600 sublime seconds. Still, they slip by all too quickly.

> At my back I always hear
> Time's winged chariot hurrying near.[1]

If you were to see the following announcement in the "Lost and Found" section of your morning paper, what would be your reaction? "Lost: yesterday, somewhere between sunrise and sunset, two golden hours, each set with 60 diamond minutes. No reward offered, for they are gone forever."

You may be surprised to discover that the above "lost and found" statement was written by Horace Mann over a century ago. That little bit of information may not be on one of the cards of your "Trivia" game, but it does remind us that the

---

1. Andrew Marvell, *Upon Appleton House, To My Lord Fairfax,* lxxiii.

loss of time is not limited to our pressure-cooker generation. And we'd all like to be able to say and mean what Jonathan Edwards, leader of the "Great Awakening" in 1734–35, wrote in his *Resolutions*. "Resolved: never to lose one moment, but to improve it in the most profitable way." Edwards wrote that before his twentieth birthday. Not a bad motto for us at any age. Discovering how to do it is not only a challenge for daily living, but one of the most crucial aspects of following the other Jesus.

A Hard Saying about Time

One of Jesus' hard sayings deals with the misuse of time. When we understand its application for us today, it becomes the secret of making the most of our lifetime in time, the most of every opportunity. It also introduces us to a consideration of the different words for time used in the New Testament.

"When you see a cloud rising out of the west," Jesus said pointedly, "immediately you say 'a shower is coming'; and so it is. And when you see a south wind you say, 'there will be hot weather' and there is. Hypocrites! You can discern the face of the sky and the weather, but how is it you do not discern this time?" (Luke 12:54–56).

The Jews were able to determine the weather conditions by the cloud formations in the sky and the direction of the wind, but were not able to grasp the special time in which they were living. Their Messiah had come, and yet they were unable to read the signs of the times. Matthew's version of Jesus' hard saying underlines that even more forcefully: "Hypocrites! You know how to discern the face of the sky, but you cannot discern the signs of the times" (Matt. 16:3).

We are taken aback by the word "hypocrites." It means

"to play a part, to go double, to pretend, to be one thing on the outside but something very different on the inside." Actually, Jesus was accusing the people of unwillingness. They were pretending they didn't understand what was happening through His ministry. The long-awaited Messiah was in their midst doing exactly what the prophets had predicted, and yet they were unwilling to accept Him.

Earlier, when Jesus had read Isaiah 61:1–2 in the synagogue in Nazareth, He had said, "Today this Scripture is fulfilled in your hearing" (Luke 4:21). With provincial faithlessness, some of the people responded, "Is not this Joseph's son?" It was difficult for many of them to accept that one from their own hometown could make such messianic claims. Others were filled with wrath and threw Jesus out of Nazareth and tried to cast Him over a cliff. Miraculously, He escaped their violent intent to kill Him.

The people to whom Jesus spoke the hard saying that we are considering in this chapter didn't react with such violence. They were too busy fussing about the weather to focus on the central event of all time which was taking place in their time. Many of us can identify with that. Sometimes we are more concerned about the weather reports than we are about what the Lord may have planned for us, rain or shine.

I remember a time when our church planned to hold our Easter services in the Hollywood Bowl. Some of our people were very concerned over the possibility of rain. "What if we lose all the money we've invested in renting the Bowl and in all the preparations?"

Friends in the weather forecasting business were consulted. Even though sunshine was forecast, several people insisted that we should buy foul weather insurance. They seemed more concerned about the possibility of rain than the celebration of the Resurrection. One man, reacting to all the worry, said, "Listen, if we can't put up umbrellas and sing 'Hallelujah, Christ is risen!' we're not much of a church. Saints don't melt. Let's focus on the momentous thing which will happen when people receive the risen Lord rather than on what might happen if it rains!"

As it worked out, the sun did shine and nine thousand people gathered to celebrate Easter. But there would have been no less joy if it had been cloudy or even if it had rained.

It's easy to get distracted by what might happen in any moment in time and miss what the Lord has planned for that time. We all worry about the future. We borrow tomorrow's anticipated troubles or anxieties and overlook the precious gift of today. During the passage of time, we may fail to grasp the opportunities of the never-to-be-repeated miracle of today. To avoid that danger, we need to consider Jesus' very special use of the word "time" in this hard saying.

The Greek word for "time" selected by both Luke and Matthew in Jesus' phrase "this time" or "the signs of the times" means event-centered time. Three words for "time" are used in the New Testament. *Chronos* meant duration of temporal time. *Aiōn* meant the characteristics of an age or generation in the *chronos* passage of time. *Kairos*, distinguished from *chronos*, was used to signify a specific happening in the movement of time. For example, the period of germination, sprouting, and growth of a seed into full grain ready to be harvested would be *chronos* time. The harvest time would be *kairos* time. Or, the period of pregnancy would be *chronos*, but the actual birth *kairos*.

Jesus did not say, "You cannot discern the signs of the *chronos* passage of calendar time," but, "You cannot discern the signs of the *kairos*." Clearly he was referring to the epoch-making event of His incarnation. In Him God was invading time to reconcile the world to Himself. Calvary became the *kairos* event which eventually divided *chronos* time into B.C. and A.D.

After the cross, resurrection, ascension, and return of Christ as reigning Lord, His constant interventions in the lives of His followers electrified the *chronos* passage of time with *kairos* events. The greatest was the effusion of the Spirit at Pentecost.

From then on, *chronos* time has been filled with a never-ending succession of *kairos* events. As indwelling Lord, Christ is constantly seeking to guide Christians into the adventure of the intersection of what He wants to do with what happens in the hours, days, months, and years of our lives.

Reading the Signs of the Time

Wide-awake awareness of the possibility of experiencing Christ-events in the succession of the ongoing occurrences of our days is the challenging calling of a Christian.

You and I are A.D., post-Pentecost people, called to read the signs of the times in the later years of the twentieth century. Reading those signs brings us to the *kairos* for which we were born and then frees us to live expectant, *kairos*-centered lives for the duration of our *chronos* time on earth.

The signs we are to read are a combination of what Christ did, what He is doing in the lives of others, and what we need Him to do in us. The ultimate tangible sign is the biblical account of Christ's message of love and forgiveness, His call to the Kingdom, His death for our sins, His resurrection for our victory over death, and His indwelling presence and abiding power.

When we hear the Gospel, the essential *kairos* time for us has begun. When we observe Christ's life-transforming *kairos*

activity in others, a longing arises in us to know Christ personally. We are brought to the crisis moment of decision in which
we must respond to ourselves and accept Christ as Savior
and receive Him as indwelling Lord.

Everything depends upon that *kairos* time of decision. After
that conversion event, we are able to live with an entirely
different attitude toward the passage of time.

Instead of viewing life as a constant battle with time, including alarm clocks, schedules, and the pressures of time, we
look for the Lord's serendipities in the routines of life. Life
becomes a continuous succession of sublime moments—opportunities to discern what He wants to occur in what is happening
to and around us.

Living Life as a Privilege

Looking at life as a privilege produces a radical change in
us; I learned that secret from James Stewart one summer
years ago. He had been one of my professors during my
student days at New College in Edinburgh, Scotland. Through
the years in the ministry, refresher courses and visits with
Dr. Stewart have enriched my life immeasurably. During
one of those visits, I confessed my battle with time and the
exhaustion I was feeling after a busy year of ministry. His
advice was liberating. "Lloyd, do what you can in any day.
Expect the Lord to intervene with supernatural power, and
live life as a privilege!"

From that advice I adopted a three-word model. I say it
to myself at the beginning of each day and all through the
pressures of the day. It's become my life slogan. "It's a privilege!"

I've discovered that by repeating those three words all

through the day, I can transform the dull routines as well as the exciting opportunities into Christ-events. That includes everything from the mundane duties of life and a desk piled high with things to do, to meeting with people and to preaching the Gospel. It's a privilege to be alive, to be filled with Christ's Spirit, to see what He's going to do with the challenges in my life.

I'm glad I discovered the secret of living life as a privilege in time to share it with my children before they became adults. Before that, I was creating a very grim picture of the pressures of life. My attitudes and words certainly didn't communicate the idea that I viewed work as a privilege. In my effort not to have the children feel neglected because of the demands of my work, I would talk about it as something I had to do. When leaving the house for the day, I would say grimly, "I have to go to work." I thought I was implying that I'd rather stay home with the children.

One day I overheard Heather and Scott playing "house." Scott had my size twelve-and-a-half shoes on his feet and my big felt hat pulled down over his ears. Standing at the door, he mimicked my oft-repeated words, "I've got to go to work," with as deep and somber a tone as he could muster. I had impressed him with the false idea that my work was a drudgery.

My wife, Mary Jane, now tells me that she offset that impression by telling the children how much I loved working. After I'd left with the parting shot, "I've got to go to work," she would tell the children, "Your dad really enjoys working. It's thrilling for him. And it will be for you when you grow up."

After my discovery of the "It's a privilege!" motto, then I could say, "I'm very excited about going to work today. I

can't wait to see what the Lord's going to do. What a privilege!"
One of the special joys of my life today is seeing all three of
my children tackle work with gusto and zest.

Let's Do It!—The Story of Paul Reed

Recently I led a celebration worship at the memorial service
for Dr. Paul Reed, an Elder in our church. He was a distinguished opthalmological physician and surgeon. Though he
had a difficult childhood and had to overcome seemingly insurmountable odds while earning his way through college and
medical school, often giving blood to scrape together his tu-
ition, Paul trusted Christ each step of the way. His *kairos*-
time conversion gave him a burning desire to utilize each
passing hour by helping people.

In addition to his medical skill, Paul received the spiritual
gift of healing, which he utilized in praying for patients and
friends. In the fourteen years I had known him, many people
told me of the spiritual, psychological, and physical healing
that took place in their lives as a result of Paul's prayers.
Often he performed costly eye surgery for little or no pay.
He fitted a host of missionaries with glasses, and he also
supported their work financially.

Paul was one of the most enthusiastic boosters and partici-
pants in our church's prayer and healing ministry. I'm especially thankful for the prayers he prayed for my wife when
she was suffering from cancer. He was one of the people
the Lord used to bring about her healing.

My lasting impression of Paul is the way he responded to
challenges of moving the church forward in all areas. Whenever
a new vision or program was presented, and he was convinced
it was part of our mission, he would come to me with a

twinkle in his eye, and with a customary snap of his finger he would say, "Let's do it!"

It was fitting to close my remarks at Paul's memorial service with some lines from a poem by Roselle Mercher Montgomery.

> For us who knew you, dread of life is past!
> You took life, tiptoe, to the very last.
> To you death came no conqueror; in the end
> You merely smiled to greet another Friend!

Living with "Let's do it!" enthusiasm in our lives each day will prepare us for an epitaph like that at the end of our lives. We pause to wonder, "If I die today, would the words of that poem be fitting for my memorial service?"

Giving in Time for All Time

Another person I think of as I reflect on people I know who are living life as a privilege is Rachel Atkinson. She is one of the finest stewards of God's blessings I know. Through her prayers and financial generosity, she has enabled a great many strategic ministries in spreading the Gospel. The other day, over tea, I tried to find adequate words to thank her for all the help she's been to me in our television ministry. "Oh, Lloyd, don't thank me," she said joyously. "It's my privilege to give!"

We simply do not know what opportunities the Lord has prepared for us in the onward march of time. The only way to be prepared is to commit each day to Him. That, combined with prayer and consistent study of the Scriptures, will sensitize us to receive His interventions in the events of our lives. When the opportunities do come—and they will every day— we will be able to embrace each one as a *kairos* event.

The Three Lights

I like Dr. F. B. Meyer's formula for making the most of our time. One dark, starless night, while crossing the Irish Channel, he said to the captain of the ship, "How can you find the way into Holyhead Harbor on so dark a night as this?" The captain responded, "You see those three lights? Those three lights must line up behind each other as one, and when we see all three so united, we know the exact position of the harbor's mouth."

Meyer goes on to spell out the implications of that parable. "When we want to know God's will, there are three things which always concur—the inward impulse, the Word of God, and the trend of circumstances." He lived life to the fullest with that threefold formula for grasping the Lord's will in his use of time: the Lord in the heart creating open receptivity, the Lord speaking through Scripture clarifying His priorities and collaborating what He is saying in the heart, and the Lord working in circumstances to put us in the right place at the right time.

But even when we have all three of these lights lined up to bring us "before the port" to some great opportunity, we still need the courage to sail in and take advantage of what the Lord has prepared.

The Apostle Paul gives us some positive practical advice on how to do that. It is the key to maximum time management. In Ephesians 5:15–16, he writes, "See then that you walk circumspectly, not as fools but as wise, redeeming the time, because the days are evil." The word for "time" is the same one Jesus used, *kairon*. But how can we redeem time?

What Paul is really saying here is that we are to buy up our opportunities. The Greek word for "redeeming" is a term from the marketplace meaning "to purchase or buy up." As used by Paul it means to buy up an opportunity for oneself. We are to use everything and see everyone as an advantageous opportunity. We are to take advantage of every opportunity Christ presents and do whatever He leads us to do for His glory. The New International Version renders the phrase "redeeming the time" as "make the most of every opportunity."

The image of "buying time" makes us wonder what we use as currency for the purchase. Think of it this way. We give up our control of time and accept Christ's control. Instead of looking at the succession of events in our daily lives as part of the pressure of the flow of time, we accept the condition that He is in charge and will guide us in making the most of the opportunities He sends us. We give up a lower view of time as nothing but *chronos*, and live instead with *kairos* intensity and sensitivity.

That means living in "event-tight" compartments in which we give ourselves to being witnesses of the Lord's grace. We are free from worry about the past or the future and are able to live in the "now" moment. That brings a relaxed leisure and an unpressured awareness of what the Lord is doing in the present moment. Add together all those serendipitous moments and we have a great day. Multiply those days and we have a lifetime of living to the fullest.

We will pass through this world but once. Every moment can be sublime or mundane. Each event can be drudgery or delight. We begin each day and hour with a full bank account of grace to buy up the time. In every relationship, conversation, challenge, problem, and crisis there is an opportunity.

Our Times Are in His Hands

Once again a hard saying of the other Jesus has brought us full circle to a vibrant hope. We don't have to be hypocrites refusing to "discern this time." This time is Christ's time—a time to pray with Robert Browning, "My times are in Thy hand! / Perfect the cup as planned!"

And many of us who feel the grief of wasted hours, or the years under the pressure of time demands, say, "It's about time!"

Don't smash your alarm clock. Rather, when it rings, greet the day expectantly with, "It's a privilege!"

CHAPTER ELEVEN

Therefore I say to you, the kingdom of God will be taken from you and given to a nation bearing the fruits of it. And whoever falls on this stone will be broken; but on whomever it falls, it will grind him to powder.

(*Matthew 21:43–44*)

EMBEZZLED GLORY

After a wedding, as pictures were being taken, the petite young bride looked up admiringly and possessively at her tall, football star husband. With a determined tone, she said, "Now you're mine . . . all mine!"

We chuckle at that and then feel a bit of empathy for this bride. She will be finding a tough road ahead as she is forced to realize that her husband is not a possession to be claimed but a gift from the Lord to be cherished. That's something many of us have to rediscover often.

The other day my wife tenderly confided that she felt uncomfortable when I introduced her as "my Mary Jane." She went on to explain that she knew I meant that as an expression of affection. The problem was that I used the same tone when I talked about "my church" or "my job" or "my book."

Even though that was not at all what I meant, I had to admit that it could come across as possessive pride rather than dignifying affirmation.

It is a bit frightening to realize how often we talk and act as if what we have is ours. Last week a friend invited me to see the house he had just bought. "I want you to see *my* house, *my* new furniture, *my* new car!" he said with enthusiasm. The man is married and I was surprised that he didn't include his wife as a co-owner. And if the truth be known, most all he calls "mine" really belongs to the bank!

Unfortunately, our possessive statements not only include our material possessions, but also our attitudes toward ourselves and our talents. We easily forget that all that we are is a gift from the Lord. We act as if our natural endowments were our own achievements. And in our relationship with the Lord we act out our inner assumption: "What's mine is mine; what's Yours is also mine!"

Have you noticed how quick we are to take credit for our accomplishments and blame the Lord for our mishaps? When we are complimented, we smile and accept the accolade for ourselves. When things go bump (sometimes because of our own mistakes), we say, "Oh, the Lord must be trying to teach me something through this difficulty." We sound as if the problems are something the Lord sent, while the accomplishments are something we pulled off on our own.

It's not easy to acknowledge the Lord as absolute sovereign of our lives and the source of all that we have and are. We shift from gratitude to aggrandizement without a deliberate decision to glorify ourselves. But it's nothing less than embezzlement when we use something which belongs to someone else and act as if it were ours. The truth is that the honor we claim for ourselves is really embezzled glory that rightfully belongs to God.

Autobiography of a Parade

That was a basic problem of the leaders of Israel and the central issue the other Jesus brought to a focus when He rode triumphantly into Jerusalem at the beginning of Holy Week. The crowds swirled around Him, chanting, "Hosanna to the Son of David! / 'Blessed is He who comes in the name of the Lord!' / Hosanna in the highest!" (Matt. 21:9, quoted from Ps. 118:25–26). But Jesus' enemies among the leadership of Israel saw the event of that day as an invasion of their vested interests and their controlling power. Jerusalem, they thought, was their city, the center of their authority.

On the following Tuesday, Jesus spoke a parable that I like to call the autobiography of a parade. It was His own interpretation of His ministry and of His triumphant procession into the Holy City.

I like Matthew's version of the parable. It ends with a hard saying that is among the most difficult of Jesus' sayings. Many of Jesus' very challenging hard sayings were spoken during His last week in Jerusalem, but none is more mind-stretching than the one that concludes the parable of the land-owner: "Therefore I say to you, the kingdom of God will be taken from you and given to a nation bearing the fruits of it. And whoever falls on this stone will be broken; but on whomever it falls, it will grind him to powder" (Matt. 21:43–44).

If some of the hard sayings we've considered have startled us, this one shakes us up. It not only challenges us; it confounds us. The tone is decisive; the judgment is incisive. And we get only temporary relief by thinking it was meant exclusively for the leaders of Israel during those days of conflict prior to the cross. But the more we study both the content and the context of the hard saying, the more we realize that it is applicable to the church today, and to each of us who are called to be faithful disciples.

The Parable of the Vineyard

A brief review of the parable helps us to understand the meaning of the judgment at the conclusion of the hard saying.

In the story, a landowner planted a vineyard. He then did everything necessary to assure its success. He built a hedge around it, provided a wine press, and erected a tower from which any unwelcome visitors or thieves could be sighted far off. Then the landowner leased the vineyard to the vinedressers. The only terms were that they remember he owned the vineyard and that they pay him his share of the profits. But that's exactly what the vinedressers were unwilling to acknowledge and do, especially at vintage-time when the grapes were harvested. They reasoned that they had done all of the work and therefore all of the profits should be theirs.

Eventually the time came for the landowner to be paid the profits due him as the owner. The vinedressers knew that he would send his servants to collect his share. So they climbed into the watchtower to await the servants' arrival. Since they could see them at a distance from the watchtower, they were able to plot their demise before they arrived at the hedge of the vineyard. They killed the first and second group of the landowner's servants.

Meanwhile, when the landowner learned of these cruel murders of his servants, he decided there was only one other thing he could do. He sent his own son. "Surely they will respect my son," he said to himself.

Not so. The vinedressers saw the son approaching the vineyard and said, "Come, let us kill him and seize his inheritance." When the son was inside the vineyard, they killed him and threw his body outside the hedge. "Now," they said with the possessiveness typical of embezzlers who have usurped something belonging to another, "the vineyard is ours!"

A Pointed Question

After Jesus told this parable, He asked the religious leaders of Israel, "Therefore, when the owner of the vineyard comes, what will he do to those vinedressers?"

Their response was amazing. "He will destroy those wicked men miserably, and lease his vineyard to other vinedressers who will render to him the fruits in their season." They had missed the point of the story entirely. Even though Israel had been called the vineyard of the Lord in their Scriptures, they did not identify the vineyard of Jesus' story as Israel. Nor did they see themselves as the vinedressers. Most of all, they had so completely rejected Jesus' claim of being the Son of God that they did not realize that He was the son of the landowner in the story. He had told His own story!

Jesus' parable and the poignant question led the Jewish leaders into the trap He had set for them. The sentence they handed down for the cruel vinedressers really should have been given to themselves. What the vinedressers had done to the landowner's son was exactly what they were plotting to do to Jesus.

Then to drive His point home even more forcefully, Jesus didn't leave any room for uncertainty either about His claim to be the Son of God or His knowledge of what the leaders were planning. He quoted Psalm 118, the same psalm chanted by the people during his entry into Jerusalem. "The stone which the builders rejected / has become the chief corner-stone. / This is the Lord's doing, / and it is marvelous in our eyes" (vv. 22–23).

In this bold claim of His authority as the chief cornerstone in the foundation of the true Israel, Jesus used the leaders' own sentence for the vinedressers in the parable and applied it to them. The kingdom of God would be taken from them and given to a nation bearing the fruits of righteousness, justice, mercy, and obedience.

With that background we can now take a close look at the hard saying that followed. Continuing the metaphor of the cornerstone, Jesus said, "And whoever falls on this stone will be broken; but on whomever it falls, it will grind him to powder."

A Promise and a Warning

This hard saying is both a promise and a warning. The meaning is inseparably related to the parable. Jesus had established several crucial truths we need to rediscover and live.

God is the eternal Landowner, the creator and owner of all. The psalmist declared that eloquently: "The earth is the Lord's, and all its fullness, / The world and those who dwell therein" (Ps. 24:1). As absolute Sovereign, the Lord has made bountiful, unlimited provision for us. The beauty of the natural world, the gift of life, the endowments of intelligence and spiritual perception—all are His blessings. And all He wants in response is that we give Him the glory and not embezzle it by taking credit for it ourselves. But even when we act like spiritual embezzlers, He doesn't give up on us, any more than the owner of the vineyard gave up on the vinedressers but sent his son to them after his servants had been murdered.

The servants of the parable surely represent the prophets who were sent by God to call His people back into faithful obedience and trust. But the Father's ultimate gift of love was to send His own Son. We know what the leaders of

Israel did to Him. Now the hard saying raises the question of what we, as today's vinedressers, are doing to Him. We are given two choices.

The Blessing of Brokenness

The first choice, according to the first part of this hard saying, is to fall on Him and be broken. Before that offends our delicate spiritual sensitivity to hard challenges, let's be sure what it means.

In the New Testament, Christ is referred to as both a stone of stumbling and a rock of offense. Paul speaks of justification—of our being made right with God—by faith in Christ as a "stumbling stone" (Rom. 9:33) and of the cross as a "rock of offense" (Gal. 5:11). The point is that Christ is a rock of offense to our pride and a stumbling stone to our efforts to embezzle from the Lord the glory for what we achieve. He trips us up in our self-sufficiency. Good thing. When we fall over Him, our arrogance is broken. It happens in a variety of ways.

Some of us fail miserably at life and cry out for His help. Some face insurmountable problems and admit their insufficiency. Still others are stretched by life's demands and realize they can't make it on their own.

In that light, we can understand what Jesus meant by "Whoever falls on this stone will be broken." The word for "fall" in Greek is *pesōn* from *piptō*. It can mean falling physically or falling under judgment. But it also can mean falling in homage and worship. For us it means falling under judgment, falling on our knees, and falling into Christ's strong arms. The judgment of Christ is also a part of His grace. He exposes us to ourselves and shows us our false pride.

So the first part of Jesus' hard saying is really a gracious offer of new life. When we trip over the chief Cornerstone we can face our self-centered misuse of life. Brokenness is a blessing. Then we can make Christ the foundation of a new life, the only secure basis of building our lives. Only those whose self-sufficiency has been broken can ever do that.

Brokenness is not a once-and-done thing. I've experienced it repeatedly since I first became a Christian. It happens when, after trying to be adequate as a disciple, I realize that I've tried to run the vineyard of my life on my own strength for the Lord and that I've begun to act as if it belonged to me. When I fail, sometimes I try hard to justify myself rather than surrender the failure to Christ. Then, when I realize that I've begun to live on my own strength, I'm broken open in confession, and He fills the emptiness with a fresh flow of His Spirit.

The Other Half of the Hard Saying

Now we are ready to understand what Jesus might have meant by the other half of the hard saying, "On whomever it falls, it will grind him to powder."

Another interpretation of this hard saying is that Jesus had in mind the two stones used in threshing, grinding, and winnowing wheat. One was the flat surface stone on which the harvested stalks of grain were placed. They were hit against the rock to break the chaff from the wheat.

The Greek word for "grind," *likmēsei* from *likmaō*, connotes the process of dragging a grinding stone over the sheaves to further separate the grain and the chaff. The chaff, reduced to fine particles, would be winnowed and fly away like dust in the wind. From that we can draw some understanding of what Jesus meant. He is not only the chief Cornerstone, the stone of stumbling and the rock of offense; He is also like a grinding stone that divides the chaff from the wheat.

John the Baptist clearly predicted Jesus' winnowing ministry. "His winnowing fan is in His hand, and He will thoroughly clean out His threshing floor, and gather His wheat into the barn; but He will burn up the chaff with an unquenchable fire" (Matt. 3:12). The winnowing fan, really a fork, was used to throw the wheat and the chaff into the air after the grinding stone had separated them from the stalks. What chaff was not blown away was burned.

The meaning of the second half of Jesus' hard saying suddenly becomes clear—perhaps too clear for some. Jesus' intent is the same today as it was when He first spoke this saying to the religious leaders of Israel. The wheat represents those who follow Him in complete trust and commitment as Savior and Lord of their lives. The chaff, then and now, symbolizes those who refuse to accept Him and to surrender their lives to Him. In our final judgment, at the time of our physical death, faith in Christ determines whether we are wheat or chaff.

And what about those who haven't accepted Christ? They are to have the same kind of life they've lived on earth—separation from the Lord's love, forgiveness, and power. And also, it will be a life completely devoid of all blessings. These they have already embezzled from the Lord by claiming they had achieved them themselves.

The Persistence of the Other Jesus

The other Jesus persists. As long as we are physically alive, He pursues us until we fall on our knees in adoration and commitment. The parable of the landowner has an ending sequel that was not in Jesus' original. He came back. When we reflect on the parable in the glorious light of the empty tomb and a living, present Christ, we realize the good news that He keeps coming to claim us and the vineyard of our lives for the Father's glory.

There are still millions of spiritual embezzlers trying to claim that the vineyard is theirs. Among them are non-Christians who take the total credit for what is a blessing of the Lord. Some would-be Christians have welcomed the Son and even built shrines for Him, but have left Him in an inconspicuous corner of the vineyard while they continue to run it for their own glory. This brand of embezzled glory is called religious pride.

But the Son won't give up. He constantly breaks out of the corner of the vineyard to which He has been relegated and reminds us, the vinedressers, that He is Lord of the vineyard.

We don't have to embezzle the Lord's blessings. They are ours as His gift.

CHAPTER TWELVE

For many are called, but few are chosen.
(Matthew 21:14)

THE CHOICE IS YOURS

As I walked down the hospital corridor toward George's room, I wondered how he was taking the news that he was dying of terminal cancer. Just that week my seventy-year-old friend had been told he had only a few months to live.

I had known George in community activities, although to say that I knew him is probably an overstatement. No one really knew George. He kept people at arm's length. His shell of pompous piety put people off. As a result, he had no close friends.

George was one of those glib Christians who had all the right words without the music. He would have passed with flying colors any examination of knowledge of the Bible and doctrine. The problem was that his personal and business life contradicted what he said he believed.

The man's wife had put up with his insensitivity for years. His children had left home as soon as possible to get away from his domineering control. None of them had had anything further to do with Christianity or the church. In business, George had made a lot of enemies as well as money. A question mark hovered over his integrity. He kept his status in the community with carefully placed donations. His activities in his church seemed out of synch with the rest of his life. Now he was dying.

When I reached George's room and greeted him, I was concerned to find the same brashly self-sufficient man I had known before. In our conversation, I was finally able to raise the subject of how he was feeling about what the doctors had told him.

"Listen, my friend," George said with his customary bravado, "I'm claiming the blood of Jesus. I've lived a good life for Him. When I get to heaven I think the Lord will be glad to have me!"

Thinking that this glib response may have been hiding some fears, I asked if there was anything he needed to straighten out or do before he died. His answer kept me at the same distance from him to which I had been held through the years. After quoting several verses from the Bible, he said, "I have faith in Christ as my Lord and Savior. I know I'm among the called and chosen. That's all I need."

I left the hospital room with a strange uneasiness. Here was a man with all the right answers. It was his cocksure attitude that bothered me.

Later in the week, I visited Fiona, a middle-aged woman with a very different attitude about her imminent death. Sensing she wanted to talk, I tenderly broached the subject of how she was handling her prognosis. She began to cry as she poured out her feelings. "Of course, I hope it isn't true.

There's so much I still want to do—so much left undone, so much I wish I had never done." Then she got to what was really on her mind.

"Lloyd," she said with a worried look on her face, "since I got the news that I might not make it, I have been doing a lot of thinking and praying. Reading the Bible has helped, but just this week I read something that really bothered me. Jesus said that many are called but few are chosen. I believe in Jesus Christ, but how can I be sure I am among the chosen? And if I'm not one of the few, how can I be sure I will go to heaven?"

We talked several hours about that penetrating question.

The Ultimate Issue

Perhaps it was because I called on both George and Fiona in the same week that I was so struck by the difference in their attitudes. Their thoughts about how they stood with God could not have been farther apart. The one was smugly confident and needed some self-examination; the other was uncertain and needed some assurance.

I think of both of these people as we consider another of Jesus' hard sayings spoken in Jerusalem during the last week of His ministry: "Many are called, but few are chosen" (Matt. 22:14).

It's remarkable that this verse was on the minds of both of these people. For George it was a basis of spiritual arrogance, and for Fiona it was the source of honest examination of her life.

There is good reason for my telling the stories of these two people as an introduction to our consideration of this hard saying of the other Jesus. I'd like to focus our discussion of it on the ultimate issue of where we will spend eternity. I find that's on most people's minds underneath the surface.

So let's bring it out into the open. Some of what I want to say in this chapter I shared with Fiona. I only wish George had been open to the same honest conversation.

If you were given the news that you didn't have long to live, how would you take it? And if, like Fiona, you read this hard saying of Jesus, would it give you alarm or assurance?

At first reading, Jesus' words do seem very exclusive. Why are so few chosen? Doesn't God want all people to know and love Him? Isn't it His desire to have all people live in fellowship with Him now and spend eternity with Him forever? Why would He want to exclude anyone?

The Illuminating Context

Just the opposite is implied by the context of Jesus' hard saying. It is the concluding statement of His parables of the marriage feast and the wedding garment. A brief review of these parables prepares us to consider what He meant by the startling declaration that many are called but few are chosen.

Jesus compared the kingdom of heaven with a wedding celebration. A king arranged a marriage for his son and invited his friends to come and share his joy. His friends were not willing to come. The king persisted and invited others. "See, I have prepared my dinner; my oxen and fatted cattle are killed, and all things are ready. Come to the wedding!" (Matt. 22:4). But the invited guests made light of the invitation. Some were too busy to respond. Others seized and killed the servants of the king who had extended his invitation.

Still, the king did not give up. He said to his other servants, "The wedding is ready, but those who were invited were not worthy. Therefore go into the highways and as many as you find, invite to the wedding" (vv. 8–9). The servants followed instructions and gathered whomever they found, "both bad and good." The wedding hall was filled with guests who responded to the invitation to celebrate with the king.

One of them, however, appeared without a wedding garment. When the king entered the banquet hall, his attention was immediately drawn to this man. "Friend," the king said, "how did you come in here without a wedding garment?" The man was speechless. What could he say? The wedding garment was the required dress code for occasions like that. And he had known that all along.

The king ordered his servants to bind the man hand and foot and throw him out of the wedding feast. We may wonder if the punishment fit the crime—but not when we understand a rabbinical parable of that time which Jesus may have drawn on for the teaching of His parable.

In the rabbinical parable the king told his servants to be ready to be called to a wedding feast. He gave each of them a wedding garment. Some, however, tired of waiting. They discarded their wedding garments and became involved in other interests. When the king announced that the time for the wedding feast had come, they were not prepared.

Seen in this context, the man without the wedding garment in Jesus' parable had really defied the king. He knew what was required and purposely came to the wedding feast without the wedding garment the king had given him and desired him to wear. For that, the man was cast out of the banquet hall into darkness. With divine authority Jesus defined that darkness through the king's words: "There will be weeping and gnashing of teeth." Immediately after that came the words of our hard saying, "For many are called, but few are chosen."

An Interpretation

How shall we interpret Jesus' hard saying in the light of this parable? All His parables had one main point. He did not intend for us to get overly involved in explaining all the details of a parable, but to follow the story line to the one basic truth He was teaching. In this parable the obvious thrust was the persistence of the king in extending an invitation. The burden of response was on those who were invited.

In that light, Jesus' hard saying "Many are called, but few are chosen" could mean simply, "Many are invited, but few respond." The kingdom of heaven is not an exclusive affair. All are invited, but so few take up the offer. Another way to put it is: "Many are named, but few come." The wording I find most in keeping with the actual words in Greek is: "Many are called, but few choose to come." The "called" are the *klētoi* and the "chosen" are the *eklektoi*. The root word for "chosen" can mean "to choose for oneself." A common call is given to all. It becomes an effectual call when those who hear it take it seriously and accept it enthusiastically and wholeheartedly.

That was the sense of Moses' call to the people of Israel, ". . . I have set before you life and death, blessing and cursing; therefore choose life, that both you and your descendants may live" (Deut. 30:19). In a much more profound way, Jesus sounded the call to the kingdom and eternal life, and demanded a choice.

It is true that Christ's call to us and His choice of us always come before our decision to follow. He made that clear to the disciples. "You did not choose Me, but I chose you. . . ." Yet the disciples struggled for three years to be willing to choose to be chosen. It was only after Pentecost that they were ready to accept their chosenness.

What Is the Wedding Garment?

Now what about the man who wasn't properly dressed for the wedding? He was clearly called to the wedding feast, and he responded. Nevertheless, he was missing the one thing the king required. We wonder what the wedding garment represented in Jesus' mind. Whatever it was, it symbolized an essential part of being chosen, for His saying about the called and chosen is inseparable from it. It was as if He had said, "Many are called, but few have the basic gift that enables them to accept the idea that they are chosen."

I think Jesus was looking ahead to the wedding feast of Pentecost when the church, His bride, would be born. After the resurrection, He promised, "Behold, I send the promise of My Father upon you; but tarry in the city of Jerusalem until you are endued with power from on high" (Luke 24:49). The Greek word for "endued," *endusesthe*, from *enduō*, means "clothed." The wedding garment is the indwelling Spirit.

Some have suggested that faith is the wedding garment, while others are convinced that it is a Christlike character. Both of these are gifts of the Spirit. He convinces us of our need and makes the cross and the resurrection real to us. He sounds the call of the Gospel in our souls and frees us to respond. And it is He who confirms in us that we are chosen.

The Seal of the Spirit

In Ephesians, Paul speaks of the sealing of the Spirit. In ancient times, after a package was wrapped, the seal of the owner was pressed into soft wax on the top of it. The seal had the image of the owner on it as a sure identification of ownership. That helps us understand the assurance the apostle communicated to the Christians in Asia Minor. "In Him also we have obtained an inheritance, being predestined according to the purpose of Him who works all things according to the counsel of His will, that we who first trusted in Christ should be to the praise of His Glory. In Him you also trusted, after you heard the word of truth, the gospel of your salvation; in whom also, having believed, *you were sealed with the Holy Spirit of promise*" (Eph. 1:11–13; italics added).

The sealing ministry of the Holy Spirit is the confirming authentication of our call and *our chosenness*. Paul refers to the Spirit as the guarantee of our inheritance. The guarantee is for us, not God. We need to know we are His now and forever. The Spirit does that. He clothes us with power.

But Why So Few?

In the light of that guarantee, our minds go back to Jesus' stark words "Few are chosen." Did He mean that the inner work of the Spirit is given to a select few? The select, yes, but not a few.

It is possible to resist the sealing ministry of the Spirit. We can try to crash the wedding feast of heaven without the full work of the Spirit having been accomplished in us. To know what the King, our Lord, requires and to defy Him not only exposes our willfulness, but also what we really think of Him. We want things our way and refuse the gift of the wedding garment. To know we are called but to choose not to allow the Spirit to have full reign in us may be an indication that we really have refused to be chosen.

The 95/5 Ratio

The call and choice of us is God's gracious invitation. He created us for Himself, came in Christ to redeem us, and works in us to set us free to respond. Our part in our salvation is a small percentage.

I like to think of it as a 95/5 percentage ratio: 95 percent

God's action and 5 percent our response. But on that 5 percent expression of our free wills depends how much of the 95 percent we are able to receive. God has made it that way.

There is no love relationship without a choice on the part of both parties. He created us for Himself to love and for us to love Him. We are not puppets without wills. We are all loved, cherished, called, and chosen people. But we have the power to choose to be chosen. If that's so, the flip side is also true: we can choose not to be chosen.

Meanwhile . . . Back at the Hospital

On the basis of what we've discovered about the deeper meaning of Jesus' hard saying, let's take another look at George and Fiona, whom we met at the opening of this chapter. Though George spouted words of faith in Christ, he was really trusting in himself, not Christ. He said the right things, but there was no evidence of any of the true marks of surrender to Christ. He was missing the wedding garment. He was not clothed with the Spirit. Instead, he was decked out in the pretentious robes of his own self-generated righteousness. Whenever I think of him, I remember still another of Christ's hard sayings, "Not everyone who says to me, 'Lord, Lord,' shall enter the kingdom of heaven, but he who does the will of My Father in heaven. Many will say to Me in that day, 'Lord, Lord, have we not prophesied in Your name, cast out demons in Your name, and done many wonders in Your name?' And then I will declare to them, 'I never knew you; depart from Me, you who practice lawlessness!' " (Matt. 7:21–23).

Fiona had the quality of humble openness the man lacked. She was willing to receive. In our conversation that day, we talked about the true meaning of being called and chosen in the way I have described it in this chapter. Near the end of the conversation, she said, "I want to exercise my 5 percent option. I want the Lord to know I choose to be chosen. My only regret is that I've waited so long. Amazing—all these years and never really being sure I belong to the Lord!"

"Don't worry about that," I said warmly. "You've got forever to enjoy Him." And indeed she has. The Spirit had been working while we talked that afternoon. And into the softened wax of her heart, He pressed the seal of Christ. She was wrapped in love and on her way to heaven.

CHAPTER THIRTEEN

I say to you that likewise there will be more joy in heaven over one sinner who repents than over ninety-nine just persons who need no repentance.

(Luke 15:7)

MISSING THE FATHER'S PARTY

Recently, at a retreat, after singing John Newton's hymn "Amazing Grace," a woman turned to me and said, "Every time we sing that lovely hymn, I want to change the words, 'I once was lost but now am found.' I need to sing, 'I constantly get lost and need to be found.' I've known Christ for years, but it's alarming to realize how often I take Him for granted. When I do, I begin to feel miserable. If I muddle too long in that, I soon become stale in my prayers. It's difficult to go to God when I get into that state. And that's when He comes to me. He's never left, really, but He uses something to remind me of His grace. It's as if He finds me all over again, time after time. And the fact that He does—that's amazing grace to me!"

The Lost on the Father's Heart

The Father always has the lost on His heart. He yearns for us when we are separated from Him. There's an aching loneliness in His heart when we are estranged from Him. He grieves when we set up barriers against His best for our lives. He longs for the intimate oneness with us He created us to enjoy. And when we wander from Him or turn our backs on Him, He does not condemn us. The Father sees us as lost people needing to know how much He loves and forgives us.

The lost are not bad, down-and-out people; they are those who are trying to make it without the Father. We can be lost in an executive suite as well as destitute on a park bench. Being lost has little to do with whether we are rich or poor, educated or uneducated, successful or failing, young or old.

There are lost people in churches and among the religious who don't know the Father personally. There's an emptiness inside that not even a busy life can fill. Lost persons can have lots of friends and still feel lonely. An undefined longing makes them restless. It's really a homing instinct calling us home to God. And until we are at home in fellowship with Him, we are the lost needing to be found.

But when we do respond to His gracious invitation to come home, all heaven breaks forth in celebration. The angels and all the company of heaven join in a joyous song of praise. They know the Father's heart and rejoice with Him when the lost are found.

That's why Jesus came. He clearly declared His purpose: "The Son of Man has come to seek and to save that which was lost" (Luke 19:10). And that's exactly what He did. Wherever He went, needy people were magnetically drawn to Him:

the sick who needed healing, the troubled who needed hope, the heartbroken who needed forgiveness. Sinners flocked to Him. These were the people classified as outcasts by the Pharisees and scribes because they did not maintain the traditions, rules, and regulations of Israel's religion. Jesus became known as a "friend of sinners." Not a bad accolade for the Son of God, the Father's heart in search of the lost!

Lost in Self-Righteousness

Only the self-righteous religious leaders, who didn't acknowledge that they too were lost and needed to be found, criticized Jesus. One day they leveled a judgment on Him that was really a compliment. "This Man receives sinners and eats with them" (Luke 15:2). The criticism is all the more a compliment when we realize that the word "receives" really means "welcomes." The vindictive leaders could not have stated Jesus' purpose more accurately. Jesus did not object; He simply agreed with them. There was no need to justify His concern for the lost. The real need was to contrast the Father's heart in search of the lost with the judgmental exclusivism of the religious leaders.

To do that, Jesus told four parables about the lost: a lost sheep, a lost coin, a lost son, and a lost elder brother. At the conclusion of the first parable, Jesus spoke one of His hardest sayings. It was really the central thrust of all four of the parables. If we hear it at all, it will shock us and will make us much more attentive to what Jesus has to say in all of the parables we find in Luke 15.

After Jesus described a shepherd who left his flock to go and search for one lost sheep and vividly dramatized the shepherd's joy in finding the sheep, Jesus said, "I say to you that likewise there will be more joy in heaven over one sinner who repents than over ninety-nine just persons who need no repentance" (Luke 15:7).

A Hard Saying for a Fallacious One

This hard saying was really a bold correction of a fallacious saying bandied about carelessly at this time by the Pharisees and scribes. Projecting their religious snobbery onto God, they said, "There is joy before God when those who provoke Him perish from the earth." I think Jesus was contradicting that and confronting the presumption of the leaders in their distortion of God's nature. He took their saying and turned it around completely. Not only did He justify His own ministry to the lost as His divine mission, but He very cleverly included the Pharisees and scribes among those He considered lost.

Based on the whole context of the parables about the lost, the essence of the meaning of Jesus' hard saying might be something like this: "There will be more joy in heaven over one sinner who repents than ninety-nine just persons *who think* they need no repentance."

Jesus could not have punctured the false pride of the Pharisees and scribes more effectively. In addition to flatly contradicting their cruel and brash misinterpretation of God's loving, searching concern for the lost, Jesus exposed their assumption of superiority. Stand in their shoes a moment and consider what they might have felt.

I imagine that they probably said, with rage in their voices, "More joy in heaven over sinners than the just? We are just, the righteous of God! And we've worked hard to earn that elevated status. We defend the law and keep the traditions of our fathers. Why be religious if a sinner can repent and receive more recognition than those of us who have lived responsible lives? Are there no rewards? You have turned our values upside down. Jesus, you have gone too far!"

A Familiar Complaint

That sounds like a familiar complaint that's echoed today. You may have expressed some of the same feelings at times, if not to others, perhaps inside yourself. Our reward system is up for grabs. And it's grabbed by people who squander their lives and suddenly get converted. We don't object to having them receive God's love, but we feel He must really love us *more* because of our respectable lives, moral integrity, and faithfulness. We feel that there should be an accrual of our good deeds on the ledger of heaven. Why try so hard to live a good life if a deathbed convert can have equal status with us? And then the full impact of this hard saying hits us—not just equal status, but more joy in heaven when a sinner repents!

A man who holds tightly to his quid pro quo reward system challenged me about this hard saying. "It's the word 'more' that sticks in my craw. Why should a repentant sinner be given more approbation than those of us who spend a lifetime playing by the rules? In my church we spend a lot of effort cheering people who tout their 'born again' experience. The pastor gets them up to witness about how bad they were before getting converted. He never asks any of us who mind the store and keep the church going. Faithful church members are not asked to parade their faith or write articles! Mind you, I'm not against evangelism. It's just that it's unfair for new Christians to expect equal footing with those of us who have kept the faith. And now here's Jesus telling us that they bring more joy to heaven than the rest of us. That really shakes me up. Maybe I need to go out and do something really bad so heaven can cheer my return!"

The man had already done "something really bad" in his attitude and needed to repent of that as much as someone whom he would judge as a sinner. He had fallen into the Pharisee syndrome, and Jesus' hard saying was having its desired effect. We might not express our feelings as outspokenly as this man did, but we do feel some of the same concern about this word "more" in Jesus' hard saying. What was He trying to accomplish?

I think Jesus was trying to force the Pharisees and scribes to think about their own need for repentance. They had assumed their national heritage as the basis of their claim to be among the just, the righteous. Jesus defined rightousness much more profoundly than that. For Him it meant a right relationship with the Father. A sure test of that personal relationship was to be expressed in humble dependence on the Father and active love for all people. Jesus abhorred hypocrisy. In another hard saying, He boldly challenged the Pharisees' and scribes' assumption that they were the righteous. "Tax collectors and harlots enter the kingdom of God before you" (Matt. 21:31).

The point is that the religious leaders had lost their sense of need of God. That's why they were as lost as those they judged so severely.

A Need We Never Outgrow

We never outgrow our need to repent. The Greek word for repentance in Jesus' hard saying is *metanoia*, meaning "afterthought, a change of mind, a turning around and moving in a new direction." When we become Christians, we change our minds about God and ourselves. The great afterthought of a life of independence, resisting His love, brings us to the need for a dramatic turnaround. Instead of running away from God, we turn around and run to Him. With accepting arms, He receives us, and a new life begins. And yet every day ends with its own particular afterthoughts about what we've said and done that contradicts what we believe. That brings us to repentance again and again, and a renewal of our relationship with the Father.

Added to this, the Christian life is an active growth in the Father's grace. As He works in us to develop our family likeness as His daughters and sons, we realize how much of our lives is still separated from Him and needs to be found. No day should go by without discovering more of ourselves to give to Him and more about Him to praise. Repentance is simply confessing our longing to have everything right with Him. That brings us to our knees in honest, open willingness to have Him show us areas in our thinking, attitudes, and relationships that need to be turned over to Him and transformed by His love.

They're Singing Your Song!

We miss the Father's party when we are not continually amazed that He has found us, and do not, out of gratitude, want to serve Him. Heaven stands poised to sing a new song of joy over us every day and every hour. The rejoicing that began when we first repented and became Christians swells with greater delight each time we take a new step of confidence and courageous faith.

Does that contradict Jesus' reference to the just who need no repentance? Some suggest that He meant initial repentance, with no need after that for further repentance. But that would be inconsistent with His persistent call for repentance from all of Israel throughout His ministry.

A sure way to know we've been found is that we long to rejoice with the Father over others who are found. We become so busy sharing the searching heart of God over the lost around us that we have little time to sit around waiting to hear our song. The only satisfaction that's greater than having heaven rejoice over us is to rejoice over others who have been brought home to the heart of God.

It's awesome to know that we can bring pleasure to the Father. And His greatest joy—even greater than His joy at a repentant sinner's first response to His love—comes when we allow our hearts to beat at one with the rhythms of His heart of concern over people who do not know Him.

Now we are at the core of the meaning of this hard saying. Almost everyone knows that the Pharisees and the scribes were not the darlings of the Almighty. They were committing a sin much more serious than were the sinners they condemned. The sin of not caring about the lost really disqualified them from being among the just. If they repented of that, the joy of heaven would exceed even the "more joy" expressed for the one lost who repented. The same is true for us!

Free of the Fatigue of the Familiar

Suddenly we are ready to hear with new ears Jesus' parables of the lost. When we hear them as Jesus' own exposition of this hard saying, we can realize that they are our own biography. We no longer skip over them because they are so familiar.

But Jesus has done the impossible—with His hard saying He has infused the fatigue of familiarity with wide-awake alertness. He has prepared us to hear the parables of the lost as the good news of reclamation. It dawns on us that the lost things and people of the parables were not ownerless objects or persons who happened to be found by chance. They were valued possessions and cherished loved ones needing reclamation. And that makes the parables so very personal to us. We are not only reminded of the fact that we belong to God, but that repeatedly we need to be reclaimed when we lose intimate contact with Him. The four parables describe how that happens and what He does about it.

Infinite Care for Individuals

The parable of the lost sheep reminds us that the Father cares about individuals. In Christ, the Good Shepherd, He watches over His beloved flock as a whole, but when one wanders away, He sets out in a relentless search.

The lost sheep nibbled its way from the flock and the shepherd. Its total concentration was on self-satisfaction. One green pasture led to another. The drift was not deliberate. Having taken its eyes off the shepherd, the sheep did not know how far away it had gone. Eventually it was in danger.

Don't forget that the sheep still belonged to the shepherd. We too belong to the Lord regardless of how far we wander from Him. We wander away in so many different ways. We get busy with our own concerns and pressures. We think a lot about ourselves and what we want. The lust for the green pastures of success for our own glory entices us. At no point do we renounce our faith; it simply has less meaning for us on a daily and hourly basis. And then some difficulty or crisis hits us and we discover that we have drifted into danger. We realize we can't face life without the Lord. The loneliness we feel without the Good Shepherd is our own inner experience of His search for us. Our cry for His help is our response to His call to us. It's then that we too hear the tender words Pascal heard from the Searching Shepherd, "Thou wouldest not be searching for Me, hadst I not found thee." Our longing for Him is a result of His presence with us and His particularized, individual care for us.

And when the Lord finds us in our need, we are amazed at His individual care for us. In our impersonal, computerized society, where we are one of billions of numbers rather than persons, we need to know not only that He understands and cares about us, but that He both motivates our plea for help and answers it. And in that moment of reclamation, we feel that we are the total focus of His concern. It's then that Jesus' picture of His ministry as the Good Shepherd has personal impact. We have the awesome sense of being the one lost sheep and that He has put aside all other concerns to go out and find us. It happens often, and each time He refinds us, there is joy in heaven.

Our Value to the Lord

The parable of the lost coin presses home the same basic truth, but with a special emphasis on our value to the Lord. "What woman, having silver coins, if she loses one coin, does not light a lamp, sweep the house, and search carefully until she finds it?" (Luke 15:8). Note again—the coin belonged to the woman. It did not stop being hers while it was lost. Its value spurred her on in a relentless search. Luke tells us that the coin was a Greek drachma, of equal value to a Roman denarius, the daily wage of a laborer—about twenty cents in our money. That would be quite a loss for most people in Jesus' day. But the monetary value of the coin is not the point.

Greek drachmas were not usable currency in Palestine at that time. Sometimes, however, they were used as part of a very significant piece of jewelry called a semedi, worn by women in Jesus' day. It was made up of ten coins and worn in the hair or as a necklace. Like a wedding ring today, it was given by the groom at the time of marriage and signified a woman's marriage relationship. The loss of one of the coins would be very traumatic. No wonder the woman in Jesus' parable searched so feverishly. The coin meant everything to her. And a lost coin would not be easy to find in a house in Palestine. The floor was hardened clay overlaid with straw. Imagine the sifting of the straw and dirt, then the careful sweeping. The coin had to be found!

With this background, we can identify with the excitement and delight the woman felt when she found the coin. She called all of her friends and neighbors together for a celebration, saying, "Rejoice with me, for I have found the piece which I lost!" (Luke 15:9).

And stressing the central point of the parable, Jesus said, "Likewise, I say to you, there is joy in the presence of the angels of God over one sinner who repents." Once again Jesus used a comparison to establish a crucial truth: if a woman will search persistently for a lost coin, how much more does God search for us?

Along with that basic thrust, I wonder if Jesus didn't want to stress that the coin was lost because of the woman's carelessness. Many of us are lost because of the carelessness of others. What they do and say can make us bitter about life, and sometimes, even God. The same can be true of our relationship with others. What we do and say can so contradict our pious words that we put people off. Or, they may see so little evidence in us of what Christ has done for us that they do not take Him seriously.

Perhaps Jesus had in mind the careless attitudes of the Pharisees and scribes toward the lost. They didn't care about people as much as the woman cared about the lost coin. And suddenly Jesus puts the question to us, "How much do you care about people? More than you would care if you lost your most valued possession?" There's only one way to care that much. It is constantly to rediscover how much the Lord cares for us. Repeated experiences of being found by Him make us more sensitive to people who desperately need Him. Then we long to be to others what He has been to us. Without a consistent flow of fresh grace we become dry and brittle, negative and judgmental. We become contemporary Pharisees and scribes living in the far country of the heart.

Two Far Countries

The parable of the two sons could be called the parable of the two far countries. The younger son took his inheritance and left his father for a far country. The elder brother stayed at home with the father, but lived in a far country in his heart. Both sons were lost and both were in rebellion against their father. How the father in the parable dealt with both sons is Jesus' climax to His explanation of His hard saying. His target was the elder brothers among the Pharisees and scribes. He held a mirror before them so that they could see themselves as God saw them. The parable of the younger son prepares us for what Jesus really wanted to depict about the elder brother. As He sets the stage we are given the Gospel in miniature. Many of us have known a far country of rebellion like this younger son, the prodigal. Looking back, we are astonished at the freedom the Lord gave us. But what we could never get free of was our homesickness for Him. The memory of His love made us see how lost we were and how much we wanted to come home to Him again. And like the father in the parable, He comes running to us each time we return. We know the joy of the Father's party. And the wonder of it all is that the celebration is for us!

The startling thing is how quickly we forget, and how soon we take on the attitude of the elder brother. We find plenty of role models for that. Churches are filled with elder brothers. Some have a short memory of what it was like to be in some far country, repent, and receive the Father's grace. Others have never repented. They have been religious all of their lives. There's been no party for them. How could there be? The most difficult far country to leave is the one inside our own hearts. It's also a parched land devoid of the flowers of gratitude.

The elder brother of Jesus' parable was not grateful for all that his father had given him. According to the Deuteronomic law, when an inheritance was divided, the firstborn was to be given a double measure. That means the elder brother was given two-thirds of the father's inheritance. All the land, cattle, and other assets were his to use as a gift from his father. Even then, he complained with bitterness when the father welcomed home his brother and gave a party to express his joy. He would not join in the celebration.

We feel the pathos of the father's heart as he realized his elder son did not share his love or joy. "Son, you are always with me, and all that I have is yours. It was right that we should make merry and be glad, for your brother was dead and is alive again, and was lost and is found" (Luke 15:31b–32).

The heartbreak of the father over the elder son was more excruciating than his pain when his younger son left home. The elder son's attitude to his brother indicated that he had never really been at home.

Just imagine what might have happened if the younger son had met his brother on his way home! He would never have made it to his father. Nothing in the far country was as bad as the bitter, judgmental self-righteousness of his older brother.

That makes us wonder about how many people returning to the Father have been met at the pass by elder brother types of both sexes and of all ages in their families, among their friends, and in the church. That makes us wonder about ourselves.

—Do we affirm or contradict the Father's heart?

—Would anyone want to go all the way home to the Father because of the welcoming love and acceptance we communicate?

—Are we willing to walk with others and reintroduce them to the Father?

A Welcome-Home Party

About every eight weeks, our church in Hollywood receives new members. It's like Christmas as we receive the Lord's gifts of new people. Many of them were "met at the pass" by one of our members and encouraged to come home to the church with him or her. Others who came to visit initially as a result of our radio and television ministry were welcomed by some member who reached out with love and followed up on them personally. Our eight-week inquirers' class taught by one of our pastors, Scott Erdman, prepares those who are ready to join. Then all of them are given a "guardian angel" to stay close to them to help them grow in their new or renewed relationship with the Lord. On the Sunday the new members are received before the congregation in the worship service, the guardian angels stand with them. The joy on the faces of the new Christians as they confess their faith in Christ and are baptized is exceeded only by the joy on the faces of the guardian angels.

At the conclusion of the reception, we hold hands and sing "We Are One in the Bond of Love." Then, with what another one of our pastors, Ralph Osborne, calls the "laying on of hugs," each new member is embraced warmly. The whole congregation is caught up in the celebration. I think it's something like what is going on in heaven. Our voices are joined with the angels in joy over lost people who have been found.

Christ is our example of what it means to be an authentic elder brother. He was a servant who called us to servanthood. He washed the disciples' feet and called us to wash the feet of the world in humble kindness and involvement in people's needs. As God's heart with us, He stood at the pass at Calvary to die for our sins. He is a friend of sinners, but sublimely, the Savior of sinners. And now, as our indwelling Lord, He seeks to make us like Himself in character, attitude, and unqualified love for others. Each time we repent of anything that stands in the way of that, all of heaven rejoices and our Father is pleased. Through His Son, He is making us into sons and daughters who can share His likeness in His family.

Early in my ministry I had the privilege of reintroducing a father and son. They had been separated during the aftermath of World War II. The father had not seen his son for twelve years. After they got reacquainted, the father came to see me. He could not contain his joy. "My son is just like me!" he said. "He looks like me, acts like me, and best of all, we think alike. What more can a father ask?"

That's all our Heavenly Father asks. And the other Jesus keeps on challenging and encouraging us until it is true. He doesn't want us to miss the Father's party!

CHAPTER FOURTEEN

And Jesus said to Simon, "Do not be afraid. From now on you will catch men."
(*Luke 5:10*)

Jesus said to them, "Children, have you any fish?"
(*John 21:5,* RSV)

WHERE ARE YOUR FISH?

Recently, my wife, Mary Jane, and I enjoyed a week of vacation at a fly-fishing lodge. It was fun to spend our days fishing on the river and our evenings with the other guests. Over dinner and around the fire late into the evenings, we all bragged about our favorite flies and swapped exaggerated fish stories. For a whole week we lived and talked fishing.

One of the guests I met that week was Tom. He was the best-equipped fisherman I ever met. His tackle box was filled with hundreds of exotic flies, and he had fishing poles and reels of all sizes and weights. He was an enthusiastic participant in our late evening conversations about fishing. Tom really looked, acted, and talked like a fisherman. And we learned that he spent a full month at the lodge every summer.

But during the week that we were there, we didn't see

him go fishing once. Finally my curiosity got the best of me, and one evening I asked Tom why he spent his vacation at a fishing lodge but never went fishing. I'll never forget his answer.

"Oh, I used to go fishing," Tom replied, "but lately I've just come here to relax and be with the other guests. Fishermen are some of the finest people in the world. I enjoy talking to them and hearing their stories about fish they've caught. And one of these days, who knows, I'll probably go back on the river to fish."

Here was a fisherman who didn't fish! Imagine if you can, having time to fish and owning all that exotic equipment—and still never dropping a hook into the water! As I've thought about Tom since our conversation, I've decided there is just no way he can be called a fisherman.

Then, in my imagination, I pictured a fishing lodge where all of the guests were like Tom. Think of it! Fish jumping in the river just waiting to be caught while all of the would-be fisherman are sitting back at the lodge talking about fishing. Ridiculous? Of course it is—a fishing lodge where no one ever fishes.

Christ's Call to Fish for People

You guessed it. Meeting Tom, the fisherman who didn't fish, had given me a contemporary parable. Christ has called all Christians to be fishers of men and women. Yet so few have ever caught a fish!

And far too many churches are like a fishing lodge where nobody fishes. We preach, sing, and hold seminars about fishing, but few, if any, of the members are actively catching fish. It is true, of course, that some of these "fishing lodge churches" have "professional fisherman" who teach fishing and others who go out to fish on behalf of the congregation. Having a good fisher of men and women in the pulpit and an energetic director of evangelism out catching new people may give some members the feeling that they are fishing. But they are missing the joy of participating themselves.

The issue is that to be a follower of the other Jesus involves an undeniable call to fish for people. In fact, we may go so far as to say that anyone who is not actively out fishing is not really following Him.

A great deal of money and effort are put into evangelism and church growth programs in our denominations and local churches. Yet if every member of a congregation simply accepted the call to be a fisher of people and helped one person a year to know Christ, think of what would happen! But most contemporary Christians cannot identify one person whom they have helped meet Christ. We act as if that's an option, not an essential part of being a Christian.

The other Jesus is not ready to settle for followers who don't fish or churches who talk about fishing but are made up only of spectators. Instead, He wants us to be vigorously involved in sharing our faith with other people.

I want to consider with you some of the hard questions and sayings of the other Jesus about our calling to be fishers of people. That will give us a biblical backdrop against which we can wrestle with the issues of why it is difficult for most of us to talk about our faith. Then I think we'll be ready to discover the most natural and effective way to communicate Christ's love and hope in our daily relationships.

Have You Any Fish?

The hard question Jesus put to His disciples after the resurrection is the question He's still asking us today. He asked it of seven of the disciples who had gone back to their fishing business on the Sea of Galilee. He appeared to them while they were fishing and inquired, "Have you any fish?"

Now, I'm sure you're wondering why I think that's a hard question. It seems like a very natural thing to ask a group of people who are fishing.

When we think about the time and circumstances after the resurrection, it occurs to us that it may have been much more than a passing interest in the disciples' catch—or lack of it. Actually, I think it can be interpreted as a very confrontive question. It may be the question we least want to have the other Jesus put to us.

Let me explain. After the excitement of the resurrection and the joy of Jesus' first appearances to the disciples, there was an anxious time of waiting. His resurrection had filled the disciples with hope. They were told to go to Galilee and wait for Him to meet them there.

As the days dragged on, the disciples became increasingly impatient. Where was Jesus now? Had He returned to the Father as He said He would before coming back to be with them forever? And what were they supposed to do in the meantime?

As these questions tumbled about in the disciples' minds, their impatience turned into discouragement. After three years with Jesus, they knew one thing for sure—life without Him was no life at all!

Impetuous Peter, who always wanted everything yesterday, decided there was nothing to do but return to life as it had been—back to the dull routines of fishing for fish on the Sea of Galilee. Heavy with the weight of shattered dreams, he said, "I'm going fishing." He had to do something to deal with the ache of the memory of his denials of Jesus the night before the crucifixion. Six of the other disciples shared Peter's need for something to take their minds off their bewilderment about the future. "We're going with you," they said, hoping that some activity would relax their pent-up energy and frustration.

The disciples fished all night and caught nothing. Their empty nets reminded them of how empty they felt without Jesus. Nothing seemed to be right without Him—not even being back on the sea with the nets.

At dawn, after that long night of discouragement, Jesus appeared on the seashore. For some time He stood watching His disciples in their boat a short distance from the shore. They were so engrossed in what they were doing that they did not recognize Him when He called to them, "Have you any fish?" Still not realizing it was the risen Lord, the disciples responded with exasperation, "No."

"Cast the net on the right side of the boat, and you will find some," Jesus said, continuing the drama of His surprise visit. It's amazing that those experienced fishermen followed the instructions of the Stranger on the shore. But when they lowered their nets on the right side of the boat, the net was quickly filled with so many fish that they were not able to lift it into the boat.

It was then that John, looking first at the net and then again at the Stranger on the shore, realized who was instructing them about how to fish. "It is the Lord!" he said with breathless intensity.

When Peter heard that, he immediately plunged into the sea and waded ashore. When he finally stood before the risen Lord, he felt a strange mixture of joy and remorse. How good it was to see the Master again! Still, there were unresolved tensions between them, for Peter's threefold denial of the Lord had never been confessed and forgiven.

A Recall to Be Fishers of Men

I am convinced that Jesus appeared that morning to the disciples to issue them a recall to be fishers of men. Though they had been with Him during three years of His ministry, there had been little evidence that they had taken the challenge seriously. During the crucifixion most of them had defected for fear of their lives. Peter denied he ever knew the Lord. Even after the resurrection, the disciples were afraid to share the exciting news that Christ was alive.

The future of Christ's mission was in jeopardy. He would have to have disciples on whom He could count to spread His message to the world—fishermen who would fish for people. Before that could happen, the haunting memories of their failures had to be healed. Peter was the point man for that cleansing process. What Christ put him through was not only for him but also for all of the disciples. And what He asked him, He is asking us today.

Do You Love Me?

Over breakfast, beside the sea, Jesus caught Peter's attention. Pointing to the boats and nets of his fishing business, to the other disciples, and then to the surrounding countryside of Galilee, Jesus asked Peter, "Simon, son of Jonah, do you love Me more than these?"

Peter was crushed that the Lord had to ask. With the anguish of his denial of Jesus, the disciple was cautious in his response. "Yes, Lord; You know I am Your friend." Looking at him squarely in the eye, Jesus said, "Feed My lambs."

After a few moments of breathless silence, Jesus asked again, "Simon, son of Jonah, do you love Me?" Again Simon protested his friendship with the Master and again Jesus challenged him, this time to "Tend My sheep." The third time Jesus asked, in the Greek wording his question was, literally, "Are you My friend?" rather than "Do you love Me?" Peter held fast to his previous answers of commitment to be Jesus' friend. And again Jesus focused on Peter's calling, "Feed My sheep."

When we study this moving story in the Greek, we can more easily see the difference between the Master's use of the word "love" and Peter's responses, all three of which use the word expressing friendship. In the light of his denials, the disciple carefully evaded the word for love. The best he could claim was that he was Jesus' friend—a very fallible one at that. Then, in His last question, Jesus graciously descended to Peter's word. "Are you really My friend?" He asked. It was as if Jesus were saying, "If you are sure of being My friend, let's start there. Let's get on with why I called you in the first place—to be a shepherd of My sheep, a communicator of the good news of My life, cross, and resurrection, a fisher of men."

The Lord's Agenda

Now we can understand the deeper intent of Jesus' question, "Have you any fish?" He knew full well that the disciples had fished all night and had caught nothing. He was not trying to embarrass them, nor was He simply asking if they had caught any fish to eat for breakfast. Even when we take the actual translation of the question from the Greek as "Have you any fish to eat?" it is no less confrontive.

Jesus knew that, for all intents and purposes, the disciples had gone back to fishing for fish to be sold for people to eat rather than fishing for people to tell about Christ's victory over death. With this in mind, I think that Jesus was really asking, "What are you doing out there on the sea from which I called you? Why are you fishing for fish when I called you to be fishers of men?"

Whatever interpretation we might give to that question to the disciples, it still leaps off the page of John's Gospel and demands an answer from us today. Where are your fish, the other Jesus wants to know. How we answer will depend on how seriously we've taken His call "Follow Me and I will make you fishers of men" (Matt. 4:19).

That challenge, given to the disciples when He first recruited them at the beginning of His ministry, has become one of the hardest of Jesus' sayings for many Christians to live out faithfully today.

Surprising as it may seem, some people seem to feel that their faith is too personal to talk about. Others think they have no right to invade people's privacy with their beliefs. And there are those who have had bad experiences with pushy "soul-winners" and don't want to come across as being like them. But I think the most common excuse is that we don't actually understand what it means to be fishers of men.

The Adventure of Catching People Alive

In Luke's version of the calling of the disciples to be fishers of men, Jesus said, "Do not be afraid. From now on you will catch men" (Luke 5:10). Now, when Jesus used the word "catch," He was talking about a particular kind of fishing in which fish were caught in such a way that they were still alive when brought to shore for sale. The Greek verb Luke selected to translate Jesus' Aramaic word for "catch" is *zōgreō*. It means "to catch alive," or "to take alive."

"Follow Me," Jesus is saying, "and I will enable you to

take people alive." In contrast to the religious leaders of Israel who gaffed people with guilt and speared them with killing religious traditions, we are called to catch people gently and graciously. Our goal is to help people who are merely existing to find the full adventure of life in Christ during the years of their stay on earth so that they reach their ultimate destination in heaven. It's an awesome privilege that Jesus has given us. And He will not allow us to settle into a complacent, private faith any more than He did the disciples.

It was only after Christ filled His disciples with His Spirit that they got to moving as fishers of men, taking men and women alive for Him. No longer did He have to ask, "Where are your fish?" And He didn't have to coerce them to share His love. His pre-Pentecost challenges to them to go into all the world and preach the Gospel and to be His witnesses became the most natural expression of His Spirit as He reached out to others through them.

The challenge given the Spirit-filled disciples after Pentecost is one of the best descriptions of what it means to be a fisher of persons: "Go . . . and speak to the people, and tell them about this new life and all that it means" (Acts 5:20). Another translation words it this way: "Go . . . and tell the people all about this new life" (TEV). Taking men and women alive for Christ is communicating life as He lived it, life as we can live it in Him as recipients of His love and forgiveness, and life as He lives it in us as indwelling Lord.

Getting Ready to Fish

The first step in getting ready to fish for people is to be sure that we are living life to the fullest. Is our life in Christ so exciting that we want everyone to live in the joy and power we are experiencing? It's impossible to communicate something we don't have. That may explain why so many Christians today are not fishing for people, or if they are, why they have no fish to show for their efforts.

Our Christianity may have become dutiful and dull. Or, we may not be experiencing Christ's power in our down-to-earth, gut-level problems. It's amazing how we lumber along enduring life's frustrations without seeking Christ's power.

When we do trust Him to help us, our faith becomes fresh and vital. And since everyone around us has problems, sharing what Christ has done for us establishes an immediate rapport and an opportunity to talk about what He can do to help them.

So the most vital preparation for reaching people is to let Christ reach us—in our unresolved hurts and our unrealized hopes. That does two things—it convinces us that trusting Christ really works, and it gives us a freshness in our communication of what Christ is ready to do for others.

Relationships—The Key to Effective Fishing

The key to effective "fishing for people" is relationships. Our own renewed relationship with Christ is primary. That basic relationship is expressed in authentic caring relationships with the people we want to reach. Our witness is a winsome sharing of what Christ can do to transform the basic relationships of life. Christianity *is* relationships—a new relationship with Christ, a totally different relationship with ourselves, and affirming relationships with others—all beginning with our experience of Christ's grace. In spite of what we've been or done, He loves us. We have the cross to prove it, and that gives us a new ability to accept ourselves and seek Christ's help with our concerns. It also frees us to affirm the potential in other people.

Preparing the Bait

Before going fishing for fish in rivers or lakes, I find it necessary to check out my bait. If I'm going fly-fishing, I want to have with me lots of different kinds of flies. There's nothing more frustrating than standing in a river and watching other fishermen catching fish with a type of fly that I left at home. And when I go fishing on a lake or in the ocean, I take my whole box of lures along. That way I'm prepared for anything.

The same is true in fishing for people. People's needs are different, but of primary importance in witnessing to others are our own experiences of grace in the struggles and challenges of life. All that we've been through stands as preparation for the opportunities to share our faith. And Christ is constantly arranging those opportunities.

It is important to remember, though, that our responsibility is not to try to model perfection. Nor are we required to have all the answers. That would put people off, anyway. And we don't have to be highly trained theologians. That would create the impression that ideas and theories are the secret of knowing Christ.

We do need to have a vital relationship with Christ and fresh evidences of what He can do in daily struggles. The people around us are battling with problems of guilt and frustration. Many of them have troubled marriages. Some have kids who are stretching their patience to the breaking point. Others are either bored with their work or under pressure because they are workaholics. Nearly everyone is worried about his or her health and afraid of sickness and growing old. And so many are disappointed with themselves—living with their memories of failures and unaccomplished goals.

When we allow Christ to deal with these same struggles

in us, what we have to share with people will be contagious and irresistible. We will be able to meet them on their level with really good news about what Christ can do to help them. If we honestly care about them as people and become involved in their concerns, they will take us seriously. Eventually an opening will come to share the source of our strength in our own daily battle to overcome struggles. We will be able to tell them about Christ.

Fishing for people is really taking time to be a friend. Often, that friendship may have to be a one-way street for a time. Most people are primarily interested in themselves and their own needs and hopes. When someone is willing to be a giving friend with no demands, people begin to feel loved. They know they can count on us for a steady flow of affirmation and encouragement. Over a time they become convinced that we are for them and will not change our attitudes about them when they fail. They also know that we'll be the first to cheer their successes. Our goal is to become the kind of person others would turn to when they face difficulties or want to express delight. Having earned the right, we will be able to share how Christ has helped us to grapple with problems or to discover the joy of living at full potential.

How Frank Became a Fisherman

Frank had been committed to Christ for many years, but he just couldn't bring himself to talk to others about his faith. Still, he really cared about people at work and in his neighborhood. He longed for them to know Christ. Whenever one of them would be in need, Frank would call me and arrange an appointment. "Go see Lloyd," he would say. "He'll help you with your problems."

One day I talked with Frank about the joy that he was

missing. "You know Christ," I said, "and you've heard explained hundreds of times how to introduce people to Him. You became a Christian because someone befriended you and was there for you when you needed him. Why not be that kind of friend to the people around you? When the opportunity comes, instead of sending them to me, why not tell them about what Christ has done in your life? I think you'll have a chance to introduce them to Him yourself."

Frank took up the challenge. He began to pray for people around him who needed to know Christ as Savior and Lord. At the same time, he went out of his way to be a trusted friend. At work, he became a person in whom others felt they could confide.

One day a man came into his office, closed the door behind him, and poured out his heart about some problems that were getting the best of him. "Frank," the man said, "I know you've got problems too, but you're always so positive and hopeful. Have you always been that way? If not, what happened to change you?"

Frank breathed an inner prayer of gratitude. Christ was answering his prayers for this man. All of the lunches, visits, and patient listening had paid off. Then Frank prayed for help to be able to tell the man about Christ in the most natural, unstudied, but effective way that he could.

Frank empathized with the man's problem and talked about similar ones he had faced. Then he shared what Christ had done for him. Encouraged by the man's receptivity, Frank reviewed some of the verses from the Bible he had memorized about the Lord's love and power to help us. He described sin both in terms of the destructive things we do and the awful condition of being separated from the Lord. Then he talked about the cross and forgiveness. Finally, Frank asked the man if he would like to turn his problems over to the Lord.

"Now? Right here in your office?" the man responded with surprise. "Why not?" Frank asked enthusiastically. "The Lord is here with us."

The man was both ready and willing. Frank led him phrase by phrase in a simple prayer of giving as much of himself as he knew to as much of the Lord as he understood. Still following Frank's lead, the man committed his problems to the Lord and asked Him to intercede to help him solve them. Then Frank helped him to invite Christ to fill him with His Spirit and make him a new person with discernment to know His will and increased power to do it.

Frank's fellow worker became a Christian that afternoon. In order to help him grow in his new freedom and joy, Frank agreed to meet with him once a week to study the Bible.

That evening Frank called me. "Lloyd, I'm not calling to turn over another prospect to you. Today I had the joy of leading a man to Christ at the office," he said with excitement. "Now I see what I've been missing!" I shared Frank's delight and told him this was the first of many fish he would catch.

It's happening. Frank and the man he had led to Christ that day did begin meeting together. Now sixteen men and women from all over the city share that time each week early in the morning before work. Of that sixteen, eleven have become Christians because of Frank.

Going Where the Fish Are

All experienced fishermen know they must go where the fish are. For a fisher of people, however, the fish are everywhere. We don't need to travel great distances to find them. Some of us may be called to the mission field, but most of us are called to the mission field of right where we are. Think of all the people you know whom you'd like to have experience

Christ's grace and power. They are probably among your friends, in your neighborhood, or at work.

Before you read on, stop and make a list. Write down whoever comes to your mind. Don't set any limits on the Lord. Just write out the names of the people the Lord brings to your mind. Unless I miss my guess, you'll have a long list.

I asked a group of people in my congregation to do that. Sally was astounded at how many names she had. "Now what do I do with this long list?" she asked. "I'd been hoping you'd ask that!" I responded, laughing. "Sally, you have just prepared your fishing list. Begin praying for these people every day. Ask the Lord to help you be a deeply concerned friend to them and ask Him to arrange opportunities for you to show them how much you love them. Then, get ready. You can be sure you'll be given a chance to talk with them about their relationship with Christ. You're in the people-fishing business now!"

Keeping the Lines Tight

There is something else I've discovered about fishing for fish: never fish with a slack line. The fly or bait drifts. Any extra line that I've carelessly let out floats on the surface of the water. Then when a fish nibbles or strikes, I'm not prepared to set the hook, and usually the fish gets away.

For fishers of people, wide-awake awareness equals a tight line. People, like fish, often nibble around the bait we've offered before they strike at it. They drop comments that expose an inner need. Or they talk about someone else's need when it's really their own problem. Often we are not listening to what people are saying beneath their needs.

A People-Fishing Strategy That Works

I've found a strategy in fishing for people that really works. I call it the "I'll be praying for you!" formula. When someone drops a comment about a difficult problem or some great opportunity ahead, I simply say, "I'll be praying for you!" That may be a predictable comment from a clergyperson, but others who have tried it also have had amazing results. It gives us an opportunity to get back to a person to check and see how things are going. We can say, "I've been praying a lot for you since we were together. How's it going?" That identifies the person who says it as a Christian, and as one who can be called on to talk about how to find spiritual power. It also immediately puts the relationship on a much deeper level. Eventually we have a chance to talk about the person's need for Christ.

An example of this is what happened to Norma, a waitress in a restaurant where I occasionally go for lunch. One day when I saw her there, she looked discouraged. "How's it going, Norma?" I asked.

"Well, just okay," she replied, giving me a clue that she was not okay at all.

"Rough times, eh?" I replied, encouraging her to talk.

"Yeah, but I'll have to work it out the best I can," Norma said with a frown. Her face, which was creased with the lines of years of worry and hard work, was drawn with fatigue.

"Norma," I said, "I'll be praying for you!"

She seemed surprised. "You will? Thanks!" she said, as she rushed off to take care of her other tables.

A couple of weeks later, after praying for Norma each day, I returned to the restaurant. Happily, I was seated in her section again. When she came to my table I said, "Hi, Norma. I've kept my promise to pray for you every day."

"You have? You mean that you remembered our conversation and prayed for me?" she said in amazement. "That really means a lot!"

I lingered over my lunch until the noon hour rush was over and all the customers at Norma's tables had left. When she had cleared the tables, she came over and sat down. "It really blows my mind that you'd think about me and pray for me," she said. "If you have a moment, I'd like to talk to you."

Norma poured out her troubles. I listened intently until she finished. Then I said, "Norma, you don't have to take this alone! The Lord wants to help you. He loves you very much." I shared my own story of how He has helped me in my difficulties. Then I told her about other people who had discovered a personal relationship with the Lord in the midst of crisis like the one she was facing. After that I said, "Norma, do you know the Lord?"

"Not in the personal way you've been talking about Him," she confided honestly, tears welling up in her eyes. "But I'd like to!"

There in the empty section of the restaurant, I explained the basic steps of becoming a Christian. Then I led her through a prayer of commitment of her problems and her whole life to Christ, asking Him to take over the management of her life and fill her with His Spirit. In that simple prayer, Norma began the new life.

The next time I went to lunch, I could hardly believe the change in Norma's face. The weariness was gone, and in its place there was the undeniable radiance of Christ's joy and the calm of His peace.

The Normas of life are everywhere. No one had ever asked her if she wanted to know Christ personally until that day we talked and prayed together.

A Life-or-Death Issue

Fishing for people is a life-or-death issue. Accepting Christ is the only sure passport to heaven, and it is during the years of our life on earth that the decision for Christ must be made. After physical death is too late.

Perhaps the reason many Christians take so lightly the calling to be fishers of people is that they don't really believe that. Some hold the vague notion that all people are saved whether they believe in Christ or not. When someone dies who has not believed in Christ, his or her good works are extolled as if human goodness were the only qualification for eternal life. Not so. In an another hard saying, the other Jesus said, "I am the way, the truth, and the life. No one comes to the Father except through Me" (John 14:6).

That is both awesome and disturbing. We are filled with awe that Christ has called us to help people to live forever. At the same time, we are disturbed at how many people we may have missed because we were either too busy or insensitive to recognize their needs.

But the other Jesus does not allow us to take a guilt trip instead of going fishing. Whatever we've done in the past to resist our calling to be fishers of people is forgiven. Today's a new day!

In a way, whenever we pray that Christ will be with us throughout any day, we have taken the first step to becoming a fisher of people. He is the Master Fisherman. He came two thousand years ago to catch people alive and He's been fishing ever since, through people like us. Helping us to catch people is foremost on His mind. He won't let us forget that He caught us through someone who loved and cared for us. And consistently each day He asks His same hard question, "Have you any fish?"

CHAPTER FIFTEEN

You have persevered and have patience, and have labored for My name's sake and have not become weary. Nevertheless I have this against you, that you have left your first love.
(Revelation 2:3—4)

THE SEDUCTION OF THE SECONDARY

One Sunday morning last summer while I was in Edinburgh, Scotland, I had a rare opportunity to worship as a participant in the pew. Seated in the balcony of the Holyrood Abbey Church, I received two messages that morning. One was delivered by the pastor, the other by a radiant young woman seated a few pews from me.

The woman's love for Christ was evident all through the service. She followed the pastor's sermon with obvious understanding and delight. Her countenance exuded the excitement of a person filled with Christ's Spirit.

At the conclusion of the service, the closing hymn was announced. We all stood to sing George Matheson's hymn, "O Love That Wilt Not Let Me Go," written by the great Scots preacher of another generation at a difficult period of his life. He was going blind and his fiancée had told him she would not marry him because of his handicap.

The woman near me in the balcony sang the hymn with magnificent enthusiasm. Then I noticed she was singing from a large, odd-shaped hymnal. Instead of looking at the page while she sang, she traced her finger back and forth across it, fingering some protruding signals. It was then I realized that she was blind and was using a braille hymn book.

I was moved to tears as I sang. Here was a blind woman who saw so much of Christ with the eyes of her heart, as she sang a hymn written by a blind Scottish poet-preacher about a love that endures in spite of life's setbacks and difficulties. As the worship service ended, I wondered—did I love Christ that much?

I made my way over to the young woman and thanked her for the impact of her radiance on my life. "Oh, thank you, sir," she said humbly. "I have prayed that His love would shine through me. Unlike you, I can't see my own face in a mirror, but I can see Jesus with different eyes. I asked Him for some sign that He is getting through me to others. What you said is His answer. Thank you again!"

All during my drive back to my hotel the words of Matheson's hymn rang in my heart:

> O Love that wilt not let me go,
> I rest my weary soul in Thee;
> I give Thee back the life I owe,
> That in Thine ocean depths its flow
> May richer, fuller be.

As I settled down later that afternoon to do some studying in preparation to write this very chapter, I knew the Lord had prepared me, through the experience of that morning, for a fresh understanding of the last of His hard sayings I had compiled as the basis of this book. I was ready to think and write about the hard saying spoken to the apostle John on Patmos to be delivered to the church at Ephesus. "You have persevered and have patience, and have labored for My name's sake and have not become weary. Nevertheless I have this against you, that you have left your first love" (Rev. 2:3–4).

A conviction of thirty-five years gripped me in a fresh way. The Christian life is essentially a love relationship with Christ. He is unqualified love. Knowing Him, being filled with His Spirit, and communicating His tranforming power have been the purpose and passion of my life. And yet, as I thought about this piercing hard saying, I realized that, like the Ephesian Christians near the end of the first century, and like so many Christians today, I had been pulled into the snare of seduction by the secondary.

The Secondary

The secondary is all that we do because we believe in Christ as Lord—the responsibilities of the Christian life. I made a list of them that afternoon. It included prayer and Bible study, responsibilities for family and friends, fellowship with other Christians to grow in our faith, work in the church, witnessing to nonbelievers, involvement in causes and programs to bring social justice in our communities, and giving time and money to the disadvantaged. Added to all this is the constant battle with both the subtle and latent influences of evil in people, in groups, and in our culture. All these responsibilities are crucial for authentic discipleship. But the danger is that we can become so preoccupied with a busy life working for the Lord that our personal relationship with Him becomes perfunctory rather than primary.

That's what hit me about my own personal life as I considered this hard saying about leaving our first love. The months before that Sunday in Edinburgh had been jam-packed with demanding responsibilities. I'd been busy with my duties as the pastor of my church; financing and expanding a television and radio ministry; speaking, writing, counseling and a seemingly endless round of meetings and appointments. All were important, good things, but all were secondary. As I looked over my list I came to a disturbing insight: what we do for the Lord can never be a substitute for intimate fellowship with Him. The problem is that somewhere in the process of being seduced by the secondary, we become satisfied with it.

Falling in Love Again

At the end of the afternoon of thinking about that idea, and while praying, I experienced the joy of falling in love with Christ again! It was not that I had fallen out of love with Him. Rather, as with the constant need for renewal of our human.relationships, I realized once again how much I loved Him and longed to keep my relationship with Him vital and dynamic. His love for me had not changed. What I needed was to allow that love to free me to express my love for Him. The secret I rediscovered once again was that Christ doesn't love me for all my activities for Him. Instead, being filled with His love is the only way I can love Him. My love for Christ is simply an overflow of His greater love for me.

The most awesome confrontation of the other Jesus happens when He stops us in our busy lives and forces us to see that in all the good things we are doing, we are not taking time to receive His best: an ever-deepening experience of His amazing love.

Repeatedly throughout our lives He disturbs us with an unsettling question, "Am I ultimately most important to you? Could it be that what you are doing to serve Me has taken precedence and become more important than allowing Me to love you and enabling you to love Me?"

When we protest, showing Him our lists of things we are trying to accomplish for Him, He levels us with this hard saying, "Nevertheless I have this against you, that you have left your first love."

For me, this is the hardest of all the hard sayings. You may have been bracing yourself for the point when you suspect I will shift from sharing my own personal experience of this hard saying and begin to draw out its implications for you. All I have the right to do is ask softly, "Could it be true of you?" Don't answer yet. First let's consider together the context of this hard saying in Revelation 2:1–7.

The Context

The apostle John was a prisoner of Rome, banished to the desolate island of Patmos in the Aegean Sea. His mind was on what was happening to his beloved friends in the churches of the Roman province of Asia Minor. He longed to be with them and help them face the difficulties of being Christians in the pagan culture in which they lived. In his mind's eye he pictured the churches in the cities along the Roman postal route—Ephesus, Smyrna, Pergamos, Thyatira, Sardis, Philadelphia, and Laodicea.

Suddenly, John's prayer for the churches and the persecution they were suffering was answered by an awesome encounter with the resurrected, living Jesus. He reassured the apostle that He knew the needs of the churches and gave him a personal word for each one of them. What He said to the church at Ephesus contains this hard saying we're considering. But what He said before it and after makes the saying even more challenging for us today. I think it's the message the church in the twentieth century needs most to hear. And each of us must decide its meaning for us.

Note first the *commanding countenance* of the One who speaks. "These things says He who holds the seven stars in His right hand, who walks in the midst of the seven golden lampstands" (Rev. 2:1a). We are confronted by the One who moments before had said to John, "I am the First and the Last. I am He who lives, and was dead, and behold, I am alive forevermore. Amen. And I have the keys of Hades and of Death" (Rev. 1:17b–18).

In that sweeping statement Christ reminds us that He was one with the Father in the beginning, that He was the creative power from whom the universe was brought into existence, that He lived and died for us, and that He is alive with us as sovereign Lord. As such, He holds the leaders of the church in His right hand, and He walks among the churches observing their life. The word for "hold" in Greek is *kratein*. In its usage here it means to hold the whole of an object. Christ has a hold on the entire life not only of the leaders of the churches but also of the members.

The same is true today. Christ has a loving hold on us—the totality of our lives—and will not let us go. He knows what is happening to us and will use it for His glory and our growth.

> Let me no more my comfort draw
> From my frail hold on Thee.
> In this alone let me rejoice,
> Thy mighty grasp on me!

And the Lord who holds us and is with us has the authority to evaluate our lives. Before He levels His challenge He gives us a *comforting commendation:* "I know your works" (v. 2a). Whatever is on our list of good things we are seeking to do for the Master, the list is short in comparison to His list of affirmations. What we would shrink back from telling we've tried to accomplish for Him, He graciously reminds us of with assuring encouragement. What a comfort it is to realize that the Lord knows.

Jesus knew about the hard work, patience, and consistent commitment of the Ephesian Christians. They fought against evil and exposed false teachers. Every effort has been made to keep the church pure and its teaching orthodox. The Ephesian Christians were vigilant heresy hunters, tireless in their efforts to stand out as distinctly different against the pagan culture of Ephesus. That was no easy task with the pervading worship of the temple of Diana in this Vanity Fair of Asia Minor. But the church held fast to the truth of the Gospel and became famous for its diligent and conscientious work for the Lord. And He knew all about it.

That makes His *challenging confrontation* all the more piercing. We can only imagine the reaction in the church when it was read to them: "Nevertheless, I have this against you, that you have left your first love." In the Greek sentence order, the object is before the verb, making the emphasis even stronger: "Your first love you have left," or, "The love you had at first you have left." The first enthusiasm, excitement, and joy the Ephesian church had had for Christ when they were introduced to Him had been set aside because of the seduction of the secondary. In place of the depth, fervency, and warmth of love for Christ, the Ephesians had become so busy doing the work of the church that they had drifted from intimate oneness with Him.

A Personal Inventory

Now before you read on, pause for a moment. Think back to the first time you felt the love of Christ for you personally. It may have been when you became a Christian or in some experience when He broke through all your barriers and gave you a profound assurance of His loving care for you. Or it might have been at a time when you knew He forgave you but you felt you least deserved it. And, it may have been a time when you faced an impossible situation and Christ gave you strength and courage not only to survive, but to be victorious. Or it might have been a time of illness when, as the Great Physician, He touched you with healing love.

Whatever the circumstances, you knew you were loved, and in response you knew that you loved Christ more than anything or anyone else. That knowledge was more profound than romantic love and was more exhilarating than any human affection. You fell in love with Christ.

For some, that happened when they became Christians. For others, whose first commitment to Christ was more an acceptance of truth and less a gripping experience, falling in love with Christ came later. For still others, it's never happened, and it is their greatest need. But for all of us, whether it has happened, needs to be renewed, or needs to happen, the intensity and inspiration of a first love ecstasy is offered each day.

Ecstasy!

Ecstasy? Isn't that word a bit strong to describe our daily relationship with Christ? I don't think so. Ecstasy means to be moved deeply by an overpowering emotion or mental exaltation. Both happen when we meet Christ and He abides in us. What could produce greater mental exaltation than to think about what He has done, and is doing, for us? Reflect on His most recent mercy and grace. When we do that, overpowering emotions of gratitude stir in us and overcome our reticence and caution. We feel love that is greater than any we've ever felt in any human relationship. It's more powerful than romantic infatuation, yet it has some of the same carefree delight. And it is more lasting than the best of human love because it is rooted in Christ's faithfulness and undying love. On a human level, to fall in love means to lose our restraints, to become absorbed in the one we love, to want to be with the person who has captured our hearts. Is a love relationship with Christ any less encompassing or exciting? Every day? Now?

This hard saying of Jesus does not suggest that we go back and remain as we were when we first fell in love with Him. Rather it means putting His love for us, and our love in return, as the first priority in our living the Christian life. Consistently falling in love anew brings a freshness and joy that Christ wants to give us for each new challenge. Then what we do *for* Him will not be secondary to fellowship *with* Him.

Love Lost in Routines

What happens in marriage and friendship illustrates how the love that begins a relationship can be lost in the routines of life. I remember a couple who came to see me about their troubled marriage. The wife was so totally absorbed in the duties of running their home, caring for the children, and keeping a busy schedule in support of her husband's career that she had little time or energy left to express her affection to him. She was shocked when, during our counseling time together, her husband asked her imploringly, "Do you love me?"

"Do I love you?" the woman asked in consternation. "Why else would I do all of the things I do for you? I wash your clothes, keep your house in perfect order, grapple with the endless needs of your children and still have time for all the social functions where you want me to be a happy hostess. If that isn't love, what is?"

The husband expressed appreciation for all she was doing, but again he asked, "Do you love *me?*" The woman had become so overinvolved in what she thought she was doing for her husband that she had allowed her personal relationship with him to become routine. It had been months since she had told him she loved him, and their sex life had become perfunctory. She was too busy for hugs and verbal expressions of romantic warmth. And when her husband tried to express his love for her, she was so preoccupied with what she was doing or the next thing on her schedule that she seemed to rebuff his affirmations of her. He ended up feeling unloved.

The same thing can happen when husbands feel that all their hard work earning a living is an acceptable substitute for keeping their marriage alive with personal caring, helpfulness, and warm affection. Often a busy life on the fast track leaves too little time for deep conversations and leisurely times of keeping in touch with what's happening inside their wives. Some wives balk at that; many others endure it while romance flickers out.

Friendships are no different. Many of us would be astounded by what some of our friends really feel about our relationship with them. We think that doing nice things for them will suffice. But if we have little time to be with them and fail to express our love for them, the friendship seldom goes very deep.

On a much more profound level, our fellowship with Christ is to be the primary relationship of life. His love for us never changes, but our love for Him makes it possible for our relationship with Him to deepen each day.

Deep personal conversations with Christians convince me that the need to fall in love with Christ again is the aching need in the church today. I sense this in clergy conferences as well as retreats for church officers. Whenever I have lowered my guard and become vulnerable enough to publicly share what I discovered again that Sunday in Edinburgh, I am moved by the response.

Recently, I opened my heart to a meeting of Christian broadcasters and talked about our ever-increasing need to consistently fall in love with Christ. I suggested that only as Christ fills us afresh with His love are we able to communicate Him with impelling joy and power to fill the emptiness of the American people.

The meeting was filled with distinguished television and radio personalities as well as the producers, directors, technicians, and office personnel of their media ministry organizations. I suggested that as Christian broadcasters we have our own brand of the seduction of the secondary. For us the secondary is the means of the ministry—what it takes to plan, produce, syndicate, and finance a media ministry. We can become so immersed in market reports, ratings, mail response, and fiscal concerns that we forget our reason for being on the air.

The quiet attentiveness of the broadcasters gave me courage to press on to talk about the heady glamour of the media world and what that might be doing to our first love. The seduction of the secondary can move from satisfaction with it to submission to it.

After the meeting, I was amazed at the response. A large number of broadcasters whose names are household terms in America confided their need to renew their first-love relationship with Christ. And many of the media staff people admitted that they too had become overinvolved in the secondary. We talked late into the evening about our mutual need to keep our love relationship with Christ vital each day. Several made new commitments to take time alone with Christ each day simply to allow Him to love them and allow themselves to fall in love with Him more deeply.

One man decided on an interesting strategy to be sure that he kept his love for Christ alive in his busy, overscheduled life. He called me a few days after the meeting to tell me about it. "In my daily time of quiet, I plan to keep a log of what's happening to my relationship with Christ. I've written a question inside my log book, 'Am I more in love with Christ today than I was yesterday?'" He went on to give me a challenge: "Whenever our paths cross, Lloyd, I give you permission to ask me if I am more in love with Christ today than I was yesterday. And watch out—I'm going to ask you the same question!"

What Can We Do to Fall in Love Again?

What can we do when we realize that we have lost the joy and power of our first love? Christ gives us the answer. What He said to the Ephesian Christians is a powerful three-step antidote to the seduction of the secondary. "Remember therefore from where you have fallen; repent and do the first works . . ." (Rev. 2:5). Underline the words "remember," "repent," and "do."

"Remember from where you have fallen" means to recall

on a daily basis the time when we first fell in love with Christ. Added to that are the deepening experiences and discoveries of His grace and forgiveness that have enriched our love relationship with Him. Has anything gotten in the way of this?

When we focus on that we are ready to repent. And that involves two things: to own and then disown whatever is competing with our first love for Christ. To repent means to acknowledge we are going in the wrong direction and then turn around and go in a new direction. To overcome the seduction of the secondary we need to admit that our love for Christ has become perfunctory and cold and to confess to Him our need to receive a fresh infilling of His Spirit.

The First Works

Then, with renewed love for Christ, we are free to "do the first works." For me, that means doing each day what I did when I first knew how much Christ loved me, or in times since when that love was deepened and renewed. After both those times, I couldn't stop praising Him. I wanted to be with Him in prolonged times of quiet and know Him better and enjoy being in His presence. I longed to know His will and be empowered to do it. Prayer was not a duty, but a delight. I had a voracious hunger for reading the Bible, and I couldn't stop talking to others about His love. No one had to coerce me to witness; it came naturally. Giving my time, energy, and money to help others was not an obligation, but a joy. People and their needs were not an interruption, but gifts to be loved and cared for with Christ's love.

Does Christ want anything less from me in any one day? The point is that all of the secondary things we do because we are committed to Christ can be done with first-love enthusiasm when that love relationship is renewed consistently.

The Needs of People

The urgency of renewing our first-love relationship with Christ is not only for what Christ wants to do in us, but also through us. The people around us desperately need His love. On our own, we are incapable of loving others with any depth or consistency. Christ's love in us and our love in Him in return makes us radiant people. There's an inseparable relationship between our fresh experiences of Christ's love and our effectiveness in communicating His love to others.

My friend Adrienne discovered this. Though she had been a church member and committed Christian for years, she found it difficult to express warm love to people. She came across as critical and judgmental. When she went through the crisis of the death of her aged parents, she found she had no close friends to help her through her grief. "Where are all my Christian friends when I need them?" she asked.

"Where were you when they needed you?" I inquired. That led to several deep conversations about her lack of affirmation and affection for people through the years.

Confronting her frankly, I said, "Adrienne, you need to allow Christ to love you and to fall in love with Him again. Your Christianity is negative and cranky. Can you remember a time when you really felt Christ's love and acceptance?"

That question brought back memories of her first experience of Christ in college. Then after leaving college she became part of a very rigid church that put a great emphasis on rules and regulations. Adrienne tried to measure up and finally was considered good enough to "deserve" membership. But she became so immersed in the spirit of judgment that she lost her first love for Christ. For years she had been a doctrinal vigilante. No wonder she had few friends!

I'm thankful that's not the end of Adrienne's story. In one of our conversations I read her Christ's hard saying to the Ephesians. Christ was with us and used His words spoken so long ago to help her see herself. She could identify no one she had ever helped become a Christian. A period of twenty-five years had been spent trying to straighten out people's theology, but not one had been won to Christ with all her doctrinal purity.

When Christ pierced Adrienne's heart with that shocking reality, she began to cry. With her arrogance broken, she asked Christ to fill her with His love and free her to love Him. I've seldom seen a more magnificent transformation of a religious person into a loving and caring communicator. Today, Adrienne's face shines and her whole countenance radiates Christ's indwelling love. I'll never forget the look on her face one day, some months later, when she introduced me to the first of several people she has helped become Christians.

The Sure Sign

The sure sign we've fallen in love again with Christ is that we feel a fresh spontaneous love for people. Our care for them is no longer a grim responsibility. Christ's love for us and our joy in loving Him splashes over on other people. The best gift we can give the people around us is to be rejuvenated each day by being in love with Him.

George Matheson's assurance that "love will not let us go" is not only comforting, but challenging. Christ will not let us go for long in the satisfaction, or substitution, to the secondary. He cares about the people He wants to love through us too much for that!

The continuing ministry of the other Jesus is to confront us with any evidence of the seduction of the secondary in our lives. That's what He did as Jesus of Nazareth and does relentlessly as our living Lord today.

The central theme of each of the hard sayings we've looked at is really a call to recapture our first love. And the other Jesus does whatever is necessary to shock, alarm, and even disturb us until we can put Him first in our lives and say with Count Zinzendorf, "I have one passion only: It is He! It is He!"